Slow Pilgrim

Slow Pilgrim

THE COLLECTED POEMS

SCOTT CAIRNS

PREFACE BY RICHARD HOWARD
INTRODUCTION BY GREGORY WOLFE

PARACLETE PRESS
BREWSTER, MASSACHUSETTS

2015 First printing

Slow Pilgrim: The Collected Poems

Copyright © 2015 by Scott Cairns

ISBN 978-1-61261-657-5

The Paraclete Press name and logo (dove on cross) are trademarks of Paraclete Press, Inc.

Library of Congress Cataloging-in-Publication Data

Cairns, Scott.
  [Poems. Selections]
  Slow pilgrim : the collected poems / by Scott Cairns ; preface by Richard Howard ;
introduction by Gregory Wolfe.
      pages ; cm
  I. Title.
  PS3553.A3943A6 2015
  811'.54—dc23   2015001502

10 9 8 7 6 5 4 3 2 1

Published by Paraclete Press
Brewster, Massachusetts
www.paracletepress.com

Printed in the United States of America

For Marcia, Elizabeth, and Benjamin
—these and all my poor prayers

CONTENTS

THE THEOLOGY OF DOUBT

(*1985*)

The Theology of Delight

THE TRANSLATION OF BABEL

(1990)

I. Acts

FIGURES FOR THE GHOST

(1994)

RECOVERED BODY

(1998)

PHILOKALIA

(2002)

Descents

Eventual City

COMPASS OF AFFECTION

(2006)

IDIOT PSALMS

(2014)

III. My Byzantium

IV. Erotic Word

JUVENILIA AND UNCOLLECTED POEMS

(*1994*)

PREFACE

S even published books and a section of uncollected poems is what my old friend Scott Cairns calls *Slow Pilgrim: Collected Poems*, for which I agreed to write "a preface" (not "an introduction," please note). I assume I have been accorded this honor because I am not only an old friend of the poet himself but myself a poet who delightedly claims on the jacket of Cairns's second book that he "writes in fervor (not piety) as a poet writes in verse (not doggerel). . . . Cairns has Religion that he may not perish from Poetry."

Now I must not only repeat that observation but enlarge upon it. In the last and finest poem of Cairns's 1990 volume *The Translation of Babel*, in a poem ominously called "The Translation of Raimundo Luz," Cairns informs us (in a note preceding the poem) that the Brazilian hero is "a devoted family man, a fan of American rhythm and blues, an accomplished cook, and a fiction." Moreover, Raimundo Luz ends his poem in a twelfth section called *My Farewell* with these words:

> . . . I am slowly learning one thing;
> of one thing I am slowly becoming
> aware: Whether or not I would
> have it so, whether I sleep
> or no, I will be changed.
> I am changing as I speak. Bless you all.
> Suffer the children. Finished. Keep.

That is the last poem in Cairns's second book; the last poem in Cairns's fifth book, "September 11," will certainly be more problematic for us to respond to with customary cheer; it would have to be, given the title's significance for most Americans, but we have the biblical epigraph to bring us up to date— familiar lines from Exodus 13:22—and then the poem:

> According to the promise, we had known
> we would be led, and that the ancient God
> would deign to make His hidden presence shown
> by column of fire, and pillar of cloud.

We had come to suspect what fierce demand
our translation to another land might bode,
but had not guessed He would allow our own
brief flesh to bear the flame, become the cloud.

We are in a remarkable circumstance here, and its rare excellence allows me to add one more extolment to this poet's achievement. I am referring, of course, to the poet Cairns and to the astonishing congruity of his contemporary stance to his religious understanding: I can adduce no other American poet who has cared in just this amalgamating way for his text and his Text.

So now we are in the fortunate contingency of having in our hands Scott Cairns's seven whole books and an assortment of his uncollected poems. This is a circumstance of a very special nature, for Cairns is the singular poet in this age of our country who has not seen fit to oblige his poetry to serve his belief, nor his belief to serve his poetry; it is one grown-up mind we read, one man's voice we hear: a contingency which makes it absurd for me to speak of service in either direction, for in these poems there is but one direction—inward. I'm proud to observe the wise discrepancy and to savor that service's disappearance from expression in a believer's art—likely enough Scott Cairns will not even know what I'm talking about.

—RICHARD HOWARD

INTRODUCTION

Silence is the language of God,
all else is poor translation.
—RUMI

Silence is a mystery of the age to come,
but words are instruments of this world.
—ST. ISAAC OF SYRIA

I n a poem titled "The Priest Confesses" from his first collection, *The Theology of Doubt*, Scott Cairns has his priest-persona (and alter ego) say: "My heart / and mind are separate as two stones." As the lines that follow make clear, the priest's dilemma is anything but an academic exercise—it has little to do with abstract debates over the relationship of faith and reason. It is, in fact, an urgent, personal predicament. Stepping out into the morning air he suddenly sees his chapel and everything around it bathed in golden light. In that moment of transfiguration he remembers a young woman who once came to the chapel whose face seemed to give off the same golden glow. The priest remembers her as "awkward," and yet somehow that girl's odd demeanor is more "appropriate" than any "common grace" because it bespeaks a love deepened by loss. But he stops in mid-praise of the girl because he fears he'll say too much, giving in to the "sentimental bent" that keeps him "blind to all those things I cannot see."

Looking back at this early piece from the vantage point afforded by this volume of collected poems, it seems clear that Cairns has been on a lifelong pilgrimage in search of a way to live—and to create, as an artificer of words—that unites mind and heart, that achieves a true human wholeness. Like the troubled priest in his poem, Cairns as a young poet finds himself struggling with a life in which thought and feeling are sundered—a condition that, if the numberless accounts in modern literature are to be trusted, he does not suffer alone. To read his poems, essays, and memoirs attentively is to observe a tireless exploration of the sources of the riven soul.

Another discovery the slow pilgrim makes is that the forces behind this division include a pair of very strange bedfellows. On the one hand, he wrestles with the legacy of growing up within a powerful religious subculture that splits the spirit off from the letter, reducing faith to didactic legalism. These fellow religionists of his youth loved nothing better than to turn Christianity into a set of moral propositions to be brought down like so many sledgehammers upon the unrighteous.

But then the slow pilgrim encounters a surprisingly similar problem in the world of mainstream literary culture. There he observes a throng of writers who seem to think that the poet's job is simply to recount a past experience and sprinkle it with insights gleaned along the way—a milder form of didacticism, perhaps, but a secular analogue to the sermon nonetheless.

Ironically, the fundamentalist and the literary hipster share a tendency to turn language into *communication*—so many messages from the past inserted into so many edifying bottles. And what does one do with a bottle when it is empty? Toss it in the trash.

Cairns came to believe that writers and readers should hold out for more. Great literature moves past communication to become *communion*—a journey of mutual discovery that takes place between speaker and hearer, an encounter that both have with a mystery that is both a *presence* and something experienced in the *present*.

To use the metaphor of communion is, of course, to invoke the sacrament of the Eucharist. In a number of essays published in recent years, Cairns has pursued this analogy, setting out a concept he calls "sacramental poetics." As he has put it in one such essay, "That two ancient companions, theology and poetry—after having experienced a wrenching divorce—might once again discover a mutually beneficial relationship is perhaps wishful thinking. On the other hand, it may be that the divorce was a little hasty in the first place, that it was insufficiently considered, that the two had neglected, for one thing, to think of the children."

At the heart of sacramental poetics is the conviction that words are not merely ciphers for ideas but things in their own right—original, raw material—with their own agency and power. The Greek word for "word" is *logos*, familiar to us from the opening of the Gospel of St. John. But Cairns believes that in modern Western thought *logos* has too often reduced "word" to disembodied abstraction. He prefers the Hebrew word *davar*, which means both word and *thing*—and even, as he notes, a *power*.

Thus, "a text is *a made thing capable of further making*." For the ancient Jewish commentators of Scripture, Holy Writ is generative—that is, each encounter with the word becomes the occasion of new words that enrich our understanding. That is why the Talmudic form of commentary known as Midrash often interprets the scriptural stories by telling new stories, not by looking for an analytical bottom line.

Which brings us back to communion. Cairns believes that the notion of the Eucharist he grew up with—that it is merely a recollection of a past event—misses out on a far greater mystery. In the sacramental traditions, the words uttered by the priest are understood as meeting and mingling with the Word that God is speaking to us in his Son. The bread and wine—artifacts made by human hands—have words spoken over them, but this is not merely descriptive language (removing the message from the bottle) but language that possesses *agency* and *power*. At the altar our human making is joined to God's greater making in Creation and Redemption. This brings about true union: speaker and hearers become one just as bread and wine become Body and Blood.

Cairns has a high view of language, and yet one of the key milestones along his pilgrimage has been his embrace of the Orthodox tradition of "apophatic" theology, which is an expression of humility before the inadequacy of language. The apophatic has also been called the "theology of negation" or the "via negativa." It is best understood in contrast to "cataphatic" theology, which affirms that things in the created order offer meaningful analogies to the divine. As for example saying that God is King. The apophatic tradition insists that in the end all analogies break down. Apophatic language is the adumbration of mystery beyond language.

It may be a commonplace to say that all great literature and art emerge out of a dialogue with silence—that the musical note emerges from and disappears into silence—but in the apophatic poetry of Scott Cairns this statement takes on a richer meaning. To hear what the silence is saying to us we need to become slow pilgrims. All great poetry slows us down, its meter echoing our beating hearts, enabling us to attend to what happens in the brief spaces between those beats.

In his memoir *Short Trip to the Edge*, Cairns concedes that "all 'God talk' bears a trace of both flavors" of theology. But the burden of his poetry has been the paradoxical task of employing words apophatically—language that seeks not to possess mystery but to hint that what is unutterably "far" away can sometimes become more "near" to us than we are to ourselves.

While theology is central to Cairns's vision—both as occasional subject and as underpinning to his poetics—it would be a mistake to classify his poetry as religious. Certainly it is not devotional or liturgical in the traditional sense. His poems address us in our quotidian experience of life: they are best experienced in an armchair, not in church. They employ irony, wit, and wordplay that demand the active collaboration of the reader.

At the same time, Cairns believes that what poetry and theology have in common is simply a reflection of the way the world is, and thus the distinction between sacred and secular is itself another abstraction that imposes boundary markers on the world that the world itself does not possess.

This is also where one can begin to understand what might be called Cairns's moral sensibility. Because if the truth is that as embodied creatures our primary responsibility is to place ourselves before the loving presence of the mystery, it makes no sense to treat sin in legalistic and psychologically stigmatizing terms. In his poem "Adventures in New Testament Greek: *Metanoia*" Cairns writes of the word for "conversion" used in the Gospels:

> The heart's *metanoia*,
> on the other hand, turns
> without regret, turns not
> so much *away*, as *toward*,
>
> as if the slow pilgrim
> has been surprised to find
> that sin is not so bad
> as it is a waste of time.

In a sense, to get paradoxical again, Cairns is a moralist who helps us see that *moralism* is a self-defeating proposition, much ado about nothing—at least when seen against the enormity of the love and mercy that are constantly being offered to us.

Left to itself, the mind floats off into abstractions, which may start off benignly enough, but which have a way of becoming moralistic and inhuman, cut off from the contingent world of our embodied life. By the same token, the heart by itself will inevitably fall into a "sentimental bent." Brought together, they make us human again. This is what the poetry of Scott Cairns performs in every line and why it is such an enormous gift not only to the literary community but also to all who feel themselves embarked on a pilgrimage through life.

Mind and heart finally become one in "Adventures in New Testament Greek: *Nous*." Reflecting on the Greek word for mind or intellect, the slow pilgrim strives to find a richer, more human definition, one that is fully embodied and which has the power to make us whole.

> . . . Dormant in its roaring cave,
> the heart's intellective aptitude grows dim,
> unless you find a way to wake it. So,
>
> let's try something, even now. Even as
> you tend these lines, attend for a moment
> to your breath as you draw it in: regard
>
> the breath's cool descent, a stream from mouth
> to throat to the furnace of the heart.
> Observe that queer, cool confluence of breath
>
> and blood, and do your thinking there.

Feast of the Epiphany, 2015

—GREGORY WOLFE

THE THEOLOGY OF DOUBT

(1985)

for Marcia

. . . Listen-through all that swoop
down from the mountains my curious, quiet breath comes:
I am frantic to find these
little stones; I am building a house for us.

—WILLIAM STAFFORD

Imagine a number of men in chains, all under sentence of death, some of whom are each day butchered in the sight of the others; those remaining see their own condition in that of their fellows, and looking at each other with grief and despair await their turn.

—PASCAL

If a man's troubled mind felt itself ensnared like a prisoner in this difficulty, he would doubtless recollect the testimonies he had heard in these sacred places; he would perhaps go to one of them again in order to inquire as to whether there might not be a wish which was so safe that he dared pour the whole of his soul's fervency into it . . .

—KIERKEGAARD

*The thing to remember is
how tentative all of this
really is. You could wake up dead.*

—CORCO HENDERSON

SELECTING A READER
—after Ted Kooser

The one I want is the one
whose nape is a little damp
from perspiration, and who
would be beautiful if only
her nose were a little shorter, or
if her eyes didn't hint the way they do
of wanting to move closer together.
One of her front teeth will be
leaning just a little on the shoulder
of the other. She will have
come into the bookstore to fill
out a lunch break alone. I'd have her
lift this book not thinking much
about wanting it, but she'd read
this first poem and find herself
smiling, forgetting how her eyes
actually cross when she reads, letting
her lips part just enough for the light
to catch the edge of her tooth.

The Borrowed House

TAKING OFF OUR CLOTHES

Let's pretend for now there is no such thing
as metaphor; you know, waking up will just
be waking up, darkness will no longer have to be
anything but dark; this could all be happening
in Kansas. We could lie back in a simple bed
that is a mattress on the corner of a floor.
We'd have nice blue sheets and a wool blanket
for later. I could be the man and you could be
the woman. We'd talk about real things, casually
and easily taking off our clothes. We would be
naked and would hold onto each other a long time,
talking, saying things that would make us
grin. We'd laugh off and on, all the time
unconcerned with things like breath, or salty
skin, or the way our gums show when we really
smile big. After a little while, I'd get you a glass of water.

MY WIFE JUMPS CRAZY

My wife jumps crazy into bed,
still wet and shaking from the shower.
In a very little while, she'll be
warm enough to dress, dry enough
to move through a cold room. But now,
she is cold and shaking, eager

for the warmth of arms and legs together,
the warmth of close breath. And I am glad
for cold mornings, glad for the simple
shock of waking, and for the occasional gift
of a cold and shaking woman getting warm.

WAKING IN THE BORROWED HOUSE

Our lips move, we say *morning*,
we say *wake*, we hear the words
and thinking back feel them coming
from us and going out across
the still air, waiting in the lighted
air before us. Such words do
come from us, and we fool ourselves
by thinking we have said them
on our own, have imagined, say,
the sun lifting past the ridge
and have given a word
to contain it. There are worse
things we do, and worse things
we do with words, but we fool ourselves
by thinking we've imagined all
we say. Our hands lift and find
the common breath falling
from our mouths, and lifting
a little further find the tender
boundary of our lips, the portal for all
our given words, *water, morning, green.*

ANOTHER ELEGY

—after James Wright

Any morning, you could wake
to the quick dissolve of a sad dream.

Beside you could be sleeping a woman
or a man; we, all of us, need

not to rest alone. So, if you wake
you might find that other face beside you,

which in sleep becomes more sad
than you had known. *Everything we write*

turns into elegy, and every elegy
slips into our own. I say this now

because we know we're dying, and dying want
some words for setting down.

DURING ILLNESS

Her hand on my brow
is cool as a cup, as cups
lining a cupboard, cool
as dirt against a dog's belly,

or a stone in a dark place.
In this world of hands
there are wet stones and lichen;
there is the particular

movement of beetles, the scatter
of beetles disturbed
by a hand. There is the certain
dissolve of light. The absence of color

under stone, the skeletal life
of darkness, of insects scuttling
over stone. The certain loss
of every hand.

WAKING HERE

This night, one of those clouded
nights that glue the sheets
to your legs and drain the hope
of sleep from you, so that even
the woman tossing beside you
becomes nothing more
than an irritation. So, the two of you
grow slowly stupid in the dark, being
for the most part awake, but numbed
by heat and darkness. At such a time,
you might believe you'll go on
like this forever; but the night above you
clears, your borrowed room
cools by slow degrees, and the moment
arrives when you startle to the fact
of having slept.

If, at this moment, you might lift
yourself to one elbow to witness
the moonlit room, you would see
that there is waking in this house
a word, simple as *blood*, whose sound spoken
clearly enough might make things right,
a word like *water*, or *light*, a word
clean and honest as *dirt*, or a woman
you wake to clear autumn nights, the odd light
of the moon on her, a quiet word suggesting
what it may be you are in the world to learn.

SOUNDING

Begin with one man stretching
across a woman, trying
to get at what she's thinking,
taking her face in his hands,
reaching deep into green water.
Her face, untroubled as shell, as
a gift of deep water, that darkness
beneath every surface. An uncertain
face, confused by the skewing of light,
a face turning back to the insistent
grip of water. This is the beginning
of a question. It is a boy diving off a bridge,
the moment his feet leave the railing.
It is the anticipation of a name, of hands
knifing deeply as they can.

EDGING THROUGH THE RUINS

Overhead could be a dark wind of birds
and beside you, say, a woman whose face
is troubled by the shadows of birds, her face
flecked by the indecision of birds in flight.

Her face like that would be hard for you, so
you'd look to other things. Beyond
her shoulder you might find what was
once an orchard and, there among the trees,
a scatter of sheep, fixed to the ground
and staring north, their faces blank
as sheep. There could be a stack of rocks
in the far clearing, marking the border
of someone's land. You might see
birds dipping among the grasses, or grasses
edging through the rocks, and edging
through the ruin of a house.

Maybe then, her face again, tentative
as birds on a wire, and her mouth, dropping
its words to the grasses, the grasses
taking her voice like a wind.

REASON

It could be a late night phone call, or a note
you find troubling the bed. It could be
a telegram you can't help going back to,
but something has died, or has
left you, and you can't remember which.

You do know that you sit alone, that you
have ten strange fingers, and that something
whistles in your lungs. Odd, the way
a face hangs so heavily, and can seem to pull
you over, can seem to pull you down.

If your hand were to change, become something
altogether different, say, a grip of flowers, or
a club of dirt, you might understand
the strangeness, might say out loud, *There, now
that's the problem; something's changed my hand to dirt.*

LAUGHTER

This whole thing got started
while I was listening to my mother,
giddy on the phone. It was the way she
laughed that got me thinking. I was thinking
no one could believe that laugh; it wouldn't
matter how badly he wanted to hear someone
laughing, or to be partly responsible for his
mother's laughter; no, my mother's laugh
there on the phone wouldn't fool anyone.

So, I'm guessing that's when this wandering
got started; my mother's laugh made me
grin a little and I began thinking of some
of the times we'd had at the old house,
remembering the room she was calling from—
the pictures, the furniture, all those things
we'd broken and tried to mend.
I thought of my brother Steve and how
we used to laugh at mom and sometimes
dad. It's funny how I love my brother. Anyway,
out of nothing particular, I remembered the day
at camp when that kid from West Seattle jumped
my brother and started punching away for
no reason hitting him again and again on that
sharp bone over the eye until I threw myself
into him, only wanting him to stop, and
knocked him down. He just got up
and walked away grinning like he'd
finished a candy bar. My brother and I
sat there in the brown grass, trying
to understand. I couldn't believe any of it,
and felt sick. All that week whenever
we saw that kid again, he'd look
right at us and he'd be laughing.

SEEING THE LOVERS

From the high window
of my new home, I can see
two young lovers walking.
Their faces have turned a little
toward one another, though not
quite enough for their eyes
to meet. Their nearer hands
have found each other in a way
that looks a little frantic. Already,
what I have said has become
less true. Her eyes have found
a shadow in the pavement; his arm
is gliding through my neighbor's tree.
My own hands won't be trusted
to tell me anything I need to know.
From my high window I discover
two young lovers carrying
themselves along. They pass
through varied patches of shade
and sunlight, and don't appear
to notice any difference. Where
I'm sitting, I can tell myself the difference
is important; I can see their faces
brighten and then go dark
with the passing light; my eyes
can study one and then the other,
and begin to shape another lie.

IMPERATIVE

The thing to remember
is how tentative all of this
really is. You could wake up dead.

Or the woman you love
could decide you're ugly.
Maybe she'll finally give up
trying to ignore the way you
floss your teeth when
you watch television.
All I'm saying is that
there are no sure things here.

I mean, you'll probably wake up alive,
and she'll probably keep putting off
any actual decision about your looks.
Could be she'll be glad your teeth
are so clean. The morning could be
full of all the love and kindness
you need. Just don't go thinking
you deserve any of it.

The Theology of Doubt

MY GRANDFATHER'S STORIES

My grandfather would begin
by telling me to close my eyes, blind
myself to what was obvious, there
on the back stoop. Then, his story.
In one, a lone deer stood
blinded by his lantern, stood
mindless before him as he
approached, clubbed it hard
at the neck, and led it nearer the truck,
where a second blow, higher up, dropped it
to the road. In another, my grandfather
ruined his back, trying to free a trapped faller
from beneath an enormous tree. In that story,
my grandfather's face turned fierce,
and his voice was horrible. Once, he spoke
of finding his own father, dying on the back stoop,
his hands like stones holding open his shirt,
as if tearing open his shirt could have lifted
what crushed him. In all of these, one story
was waiting, taking the shape of something
already in me, and the shape of something else.

FINDING THE BROKEN MAN

When I found the fallen climber
caught halfway down the slope
of stunted pines, he was already dead
two days and his body stank; he was
loose and careless as a boy. I gave
my jacket up for lost and wrapped him
as I could, then shouted loud, hoping
others in my group were near enough
that together we could lift him out.

It's a common thing near White Pass
and, I suppose, near any mountain town
to be called out in search of hikers
overdue at home. Having found one dead
is a sort of badge we wear, and one
I'd probably wear, if the others searching
had heard me call, or if I'd been man
enough to wait.

ACCEPTING BLOOD

When my brother lost
his footing along the slick
weeds beside the beach house,
keeping his balance meant
shooting his arm through the glass
of a side window. His blood
was immediate and simple.

There wasn't time to pull back
his clothing, to inspect the damage, or give
much thought to anything, only time
to grip him where his coat was reddest,
and to grip him hard at the hinge
of his shoulder. I held him like that
until his blood had colored most
of what I wore, until we reached
the hospital, where the nurse
could finally replace my hands
with gauze, and there was nothing
left to do, but let him go.

SKINNING FISH

When my hand stopped doing
what I'd intended or when
my intentions somehow drifted
too far from what my hand
was in the middle of, the salmon
I was skinning leapt from the board
and the knife went deeply
into my wrist. A shock of wisdom
asserted itself: the world hasn't much
use for most of us. Granted, it was
a small wound, and the scar of it
is hardly worth mentioning; just
the same, that fish, lifeless, wide-eyed
on the floor, was no comfort.

THE THEOLOGY OF DOUBT

I have come to believe this fickleness
of belief is unavoidable. As, for these
back lot trees, the annual loss
of leaves and fruit is unavoidable.
I remember hearing that soft-soap
about faith being given
only to the faithful—mean trick,
if you believe it. This afternoon,
during my walk, which
I have come to believe is good
for me, I noticed one of those
ridiculous leaves hanging
midway up an otherwise naked oak.
The wind did what it could
to bring it down, but the slow
learner continued dancing. Then again,
once, hoping for the last
good apple, I reached among
bare branches, pulling into my hand
an apple too soft for anything
and warm to the touch, fly-blown.

HARBOR SEALS

Kill them if you want to, say,
if you're a fisherman and you think
seals are too good at catching the fish
you want, fish that put food on your
family's table. That passes
for pretty good reasoning. All you need
is a small rifle and one good eye. Just be sure
you do it quick. It's embarrassing enough
to come across a dead one on the beach,
but worse to come across one dying.
The one I found had little more
than a scratch across the back of its neck
that sent a dark line of blood
into purple sand. A seal's eyes are liquid anyway,
and alert right to the end. When the sea mist
is fine and constant, a seal
can stay beached for hours without
drying out. You don't have to believe
any of this. I sat down close to the idiot
thing, and waited with it for the tide.

VISITATION

On our way to the hospital, my mother
pulled our old car over
to the side of a busy street to tell me
my grandfather's lungs were killing him.
I understood well enough; by that time,

my own face had turned against me
with a kind of palsy children get; corrective
boots were the only boots I wore. This dying
was something more than what I'd known,
but I knew enough to guess the disappointment
the old man must have felt. He'd gotten skinnier
than I'd imagined, and though he told the same
old jokes he's always told, there was something angry
in his laugh. Just before we left his room,
he stole my nose and wouldn't give it back.

THE WHALE

The whale was dead and already
Turning to jelly where it flattened out
into the sand. But my dad thought
it would be a good thing for us
to inspect. The gulls
had gotten its eyes,
people before us had left sticks poked into it
everywhere, and some boys
from *WSU* were carving those letters
deeply across one side. My brother
started crying for no reason at all; dad
just looked embarrassed and tried
pulling us back toward the car.

THE BEGINNING OF SOUL

I can't stand myself
—James Brown

In my city, you don't ever
want to be thinking too much
about the thing you're wanting
most. If you want to see
anything clearly, the last
thing you want to do is look
right at it. Now, there might be
a woman who, when you hold her,
gives you a little taste of
being where you want; the worst
thing you could do would be
to tell her. If you have to speak at all
talk your way around the truth.

This town will give you
a taste of real life, maybe, but it won't
let you remember anything clearly enough
when it's over. If you don't think you can stand
this loneliness, you'd better learn.

THE ADULTERER

In my shadow world, no one
ever quite wakes up, slow eyes,
forever red from rubbing, fall
vacantly from one vague form to the next.

Some days, a sun might shine, but its light
bumps against everything like a wash
of tepid water, and even then does nothing
to illuminate the place. Understand,

the problem doesn't rest
in a simple lack of light, but in an abundance
of light that does no good. In my world,
leaves are barely green, faces remain

confused with darkness. We have stories
full of unclear language, whole volumes
of wrong names. Each time we find the place
where we can stand our vague mistakes no longer,

we settle into what will pass as sleep.

THE MARTYR

set to flame, his eyes
discovering new color, a new
consideration of light
on its objects:

A guard dropping his eyes
to avoid his vision. A blind man
fingering his sightless eyes. The eye
of the needle, its requisite motion.
The cat's eye. A dead man's eyes
in a jungle. The blue space
beyond the trees, which is an eye.

This ecstatic death that sends his eyes
rolling back into his head,
and further back.

The Theology of Delight

TO BE A WITNESS

as a martyr set to flame,
his words caught up in that translation
from flesh to ash, which is air, which is
the beginning of speech.

To be changed as a man is changed
when his hand, caught
in machinery, is drawn from him.

To be convinced of anything,
any justifiable parsing. Images given
to discover a language of faith, the gathering
of the martyr's remains, which are
ash, which are the last words.

SALVATION
—after Jonathan Holden

Granted, the choir
is an embarrassment. Those faces
are too simple to be true. Take
Mrs. Beamon, our soprano, whose
perfect smile might warm some
into admiration, if they can forget
how she daily cows her skinny
alto daughter into tears.

The choir master himself
is ridiculous; the way he stands
tells everyone how short he thinks
he is. That alone could help you
like him, but when he takes every solo
like a general at war, you'll
probably change your mind.

Those two alone can make forgiveness
a nearly impossible thing. And each
of these singers has a similar story,
a sad quirk that tries each week to shape
those smiles into something lovely.

If you glance over this scene
too quickly, or without enough
real humor, you might write off every
other scene it touches, every kindness
that allows such comic abuse
to abound. You might see

those hilarious faces and believe
they are the whole show; you could miss
the real act. The comedy
is this: despite the annoyance
of grace, and this tired music
of salvation, it is what we all expect.

LIVING WITH THE DEAF

I rented a basement room
from two deaf women; they
never heard the heaviness
of their feet pounding down
the stairs, or the hard
way they called my name.
They loved to talk, shouted mostly,
bleated and made excited yelps
that must have been to them the way
I sounded when they chose
to wear their hearing aids.

Those days, I woke every morning to a kind
of conversation from above, an early
morning music made up
of private sounds, cries that sent out
all they felt that needed speech.

It was Mary Ann singing.
It was Mrs. Thorsen telling
some lyric tale to the stove.

ON SLOW LEARNING

If you've ever owned
a tortoise, you know
how terribly difficult
paper training can be
for some pets.

Even if you get so far
as to instill in your tortoise
the value of achieving the paper,
there remains one obstacle—
your tortoise's intrinsic sloth.

Even a well-intentioned tortoise
may find himself in his journeys
to be painfully far from the mark.

Failing, your tortoise may shy away
for weeks within his shell, utterly ashamed,
or, looking up with tiny, wet eyes, might offer
an honest shrug. Forgive him.

THE MUD TRAIL

I'd been walking the mud
trail, the mud leaping out
the sides of my boots for hours;
I was thinking I was alone,
surrounded only by the high reach
of Douglas fir and cedar. I think
it was a change in the air
I noticed first, a warmer,
heavier scent of animal. I was
alone in a small clearing,
then I was not alone and was
surrounded by a hundred elk rising,
or a single elk rising
a hundred times. And the forest was

a moving river of elk, none of them
hurrying, but all slowly feeling ahead
and beginning some journey
to the west, a hundred times
the same journey.
                    Miles from there,
they would rest, bed down among
huckleberry and salal, all of them
pulling in their hundred sets of hooves, lowering
a hundred velvetted heads, waiting for
whatever sign or word that calls them, all together,
to begin again.

THE THEOLOGY OF DELIGHT

Imagine a world, this ridiculous,
tentative thing blooming
in your hand. There in your hand, a world
opening up, stretching, after the image
of your hand. Imagine a field
of sheep grazing, or a single sheep
grazing and wandering in the delight
of grass, of flowers lifting
themselves, after their fashion,
to be flowers. Or a woman, lifting
her hand to touch her brow, and
the intricacy of the motion that frees
her to set the flat part of her hand
carelessly to her brow.

Once,
while walking, I came across a woman
whose walking had brought her
to a shaded spot near a field.
Enjoying that cool place together, we
sat watching sheep and the wind
moving the small flowers in the field.
As we rose to set out again, our movement
startled the flock into running; they ran
only a little way before settling again
into their blank consideration
of the grass.

But one of them continued,
its prancing taking it far into the field
where, free of the others, it leapt for
no clear reason, and set out walking
through a gathering of flowers, parting
that grip of flowers with its face.

THE VISIONS OF ENOCH

And all the days of Enoch
were three hundred sixty and
five years. And Enoch walked
with God, and was no more,
for God took him.
—Genesis 5:23–24

Mostly I just walk,

though I don't get out these days

as much as I'd like; my bones

won't let me do the walking

my heart wants. It used to be

I'd wake before the sun was much

of anything but a hint

of something red, off beyond

the east, when I'd know

the hills had taken on

their morning purple; then

I'd give my wife's rump

a little morning squeeze good-bye

and I'd be off again until dark, walking

the purple hills before anyone else

was awake, before the sun

had quite made it over the eastern ridge.

I've seen a lot out there:

cattle sleeping on their feet, sheep

scattered blankly across the fields,

jackals tearing up one of their own, men

huddled in their robes and hugging

trees. And then, the other things

I've seen: tall women walking

all draped in feathers and flames, stones

tossing themselves over one another,

dark rivers winding through the sky.

I've never understood

any of that, but was happy to look

at whatever curious thing I came across.

These townsfolk are always asking me

what it's been like

to walk with God; I don't know

what they mean. It's true

you can't walk far and think of yourself

as being alone out there. But I won't say

it's God who's with me, and I won't

say it isn't. It's just that now my wife is gone

there isn't much keeping me

here. I tell myself

if I can get these bones to loosen up

I'll set out one day just to see

how far from this place I can go.

RAPPELLING

You have to imagine the air
is more than air, like the sky
is crowded with something, there,
just behind you, not substantial
enough to support anything, of course,
like your weight, but
capable of letting you down
gradually, of maybe setting you down
without any real damage. This
will let you fall away
from the rock you're hugging, let you
swing out and back, let you rappel, this
innocent and helpful
lie you have made for yourself.

SURPRISE
—after R.H.W. Dillard

A voice calling from the trees
or a gun-blast. You must answer
and you do, catching your breath.
You catch your breath
and you answer.
It is easy as breathing.
You discover your father or a child.
You discover your god wandering.
You uncover the body of a friend. You uncover
your own body, freshly scrubbed and eager

to move on. There is a lost crowd
of townspeople browsing on the land.
Behind a cedar stump, your mother
sings and washes clothing.
The day continues, drawing light
from all angles, tossing light harshly
into eyes. There is a rain
of light. There is a woman dressed in sheepskin.
There are a dozen soldiers knocking trees.
There is a tribe of blind men whose eyes
are blood-oranges.
There is no one in the wood at all.
No one is among the trees and no one
will be coming. You are caught in a forest
like a sound; you are expanding like a sound
in a forest. You are a stretch of light.
Something has called you to an exit
and you have come; so now
you must continue on the way.

TRAPEZE ARTIST

I like it best between
the moment
my hands let go the bar
and the rescue.
Everything up to that
is just technique,
everything after is disappointing.

Just as all rescues
are disappointing. I read once
where a lost man
hid from his rescuers for weeks,
running always
away from
the searchers' shouts,
hiding among
underbrush, sometimes
an arm's reach
from their boots. He'd lie there,
watch their boots turn,
hear their anxious voices calling out,
and wouldn't
so much as breathe when their toes
pointed his direction.

Again, tonight, I'll do my usual
stretching, pull myself
steadily up the rope, regulate my breathing
in time with our
practiced motion, and either take
my brother's ankles,
or hesitate just enough to take the drop.

APPROACHING JUDEA

I am told there are no moose
in Judea; but I have seen them,
thousands and thousands of moose.
        —Shaya Kline

I've been in this desert
longer than I care to
admit to any of *you*. I haven't
eaten a bite since I left Jerusalem,
unless you count the sand
the wind keeps throwing in my face.
I came here for the moose,
though everyone I've asked continues
to insist moose have never been here
and never will be. I don't care
for that kind of talk. I'm convinced
moose can get along anywhere. And where
better than here, a holy land
for the holiest of beasts? I admit,
I nearly gave up, girded my sandy loins
for the long walk out. But last night,
I was awakened from my pillow of sand
to a strange calling, a low sound
like wind, but with blood in it.
And as I stared blindly into the black world,
the moon lifted from behind a dune, lighting up
an entire desert of moose, their shaggy heads
all lifted and calling out their one, holy word.

RAW OYSTERS

Like most things
of the natural world, they
have to be gotten used to, or
perhaps truer, *you* have to relearn
the taste for goodness that will
let you take them without suspicion
into your mouth. It isn't easy, just
as all good things seem at first
foreign to your tongue.
But soon, if diligence and good
intentions are of any
real value, you can learn
to clear a cool plateful
without a squeamish thought, you
can learn in time to take joy
guiltlessly where you find it,
to accept the sexual willingness
of oysters, the unadorned
state of most things, and maybe,
as you go along, learn
to set your teeth to them.

IMPRESSIONS

There are no words, and barely color enough
to count the passages tonight of gods and stars.
Still, I'll try with line and pigment to find a name
for cypresses by moonlight, for prisoners
at exercise, the name for a common night. I will
finger the light into language, and all the gods
with me will beg it to speak. In such light one finds
a hint of what words might do, a taste
of real light and a world of whole men.

A child counts his fingers and finds
there is a real pleasure in ten; or, a dozen
children in a field count their fingers
and there is a color to their pleasure
and their shyness at finding ten; one sees
a color to their breath.

If you hold an orange, turning it in sunlight,
you would find a color to its small joy, its love
of being turned.

A stone notes the color of a foot.

EXPOSURE

Because I am found sitting in mud
and am covered with a thousand stripes
of old blood where a thousand brambles
reached out to slow my frantic crawling
across an unfamiliar slope, those
who have found me
believe I am gone mad with loneliness
and cold. Because I am bent forward
and caught with my eyes fixed to a single
square of mud trail, those who rescue me
are careful to lift me with all tenderness.
I am moved by their gentle handling and brought
to weeping by the touch of their wool blanket;
but listen—no patch of earth was ever so clear,
or so lovely.

THE PRIEST CONFESSES

I'll tell you now, I never thought
my life would come to this. My heart
and mind are separate as two stones.
This morning I watched the sun
as it cleared the ridge beyond
the chapel and watched the chapel
turn gold, and the yard turn gold,
and the white fence, the abbot's dog,
the woman hanging our laundry, all gold
in that moment the sun

cleared the eastern ridge, and I thought
of the girl who used to come here, her face
golden in a way that echoed sunlight.
I remember best
the girl's cheek, the line
of her golden jaw; she was awkward in a way
that was more appropriate than any
common grace. I'm guessing
at a love that is a sort
of pity, a sort of love
we wouldn't have without the hard
promise of loss. I shouldn't go on
too far with this. This sentimental bent
has always kept me
blind to all those things I cannot see.

A RETURN

That black sound

from the soles of your feet,

the gut-insistence of music,

an old teacher's fingers

tight on your ear *This way, this way.*

You don't have to try

to sing the darkness,

the darkness sings itself. It is

black water, troubled

by a black stone, a world

giving out under the weight

of its shadow. The common

bruising of feet, the useless

shying away from

the pitch of night. Old Borges

without his eyes.

So you walk across

a slope alive with shadow,

and your foot turns in,

bringing you down solidly

and at once. So you go down

into a patch of earth

that takes you to itself

and won't let go.

LOOKING BACK

There were days
you closed your eyes to darkness
and, for a time, regarded light.
White light and all its colors.
The Christ-child in a basket. Light
tonguing the tip of your vision.
It was a world your mind loved,
the world behind shadow, a diversion
from the fact of darkness, a vision
dissolved by the sound of the dead.
Blind Lazarus dragged back kicking.
That dead thing in you
raising its head, its dark voice.

THE TRANSLATION OF BABEL

(*1990*)

for my dad
Bud Cairns
(1928–1988)

INVITATION TO A WEDDING

Since this is the west, where most borders
approach the quaint artifice
of geometry, so the days themselves achieve
their brief expressions of form.

And likewise, the stuff of days finds some manner
for its gestures: The forms
of greeting, and of play, the sober forms
of worship, the forms love takes

when the mind is rested, the sometimes
astonishing forms of speech.
And then, as in any formal gathering,
the familiar dose of convention—

the cosmetics of the bride and groom,
stiff fabrics to keep the body straight,
flowers to hide the shortfalls of the room,
the wooden orchestrations of our band.

What joy one takes from such square dances
is not so much the familiar steps, more
likely, what lies hidden, or faintly seen—
his false step, her exaggerated spin.

So, as you might accept any public invitation
and chance to overhear the private terms,
you might lift this book from among the others,
this sad and arbitrary book, this book of forms.

I.
Acts

_____

And how hear we every man
In our own tongue, wherein we were born?

—Luke, Acts of the Apostles

ACTS

So little to be done and so much time.
I nearly told the giddy crowd outside
the Pentecostal church they might go home
—for all the good they'd do—or spend the evening
with their own queer group there on the lawn
instead of squeezing again into their failing
buses for another dose of humility
at selected crossroads, the worst parts of town.

But I know these types too well. If I had
said a word, the tall boy with those startling ears
and disquieting blue skin would be the one
to bleat some trembling prayer while the others
quivering as if shocked would lay on me
a crown of hands. So I just stood there,
watching their sincere, low-rent theater,
this eager preparation for their war.

Years ago, I was unlucky enough
to find another of these witless boys
shouting at my corner, cataloguing
sin with an astonishing lack of charm.
In time, the crowd abandoned humor, but
they couldn't shut him up. From that grim press,
another boy—some squat lump with rolled sleeves—
approached the believer and slapped him hard.

When the witness didn't move, the hand
came up again. As the third blow barked I found
myself shoving in, hating both of them,
but pulling out the one I hated most
and pulling him to my own door. Away
from the jubilant cattle at the crossing,
my indiscreet relation dropped wholly
down, forsaking all for his appalling tongues.

MEMORY

The problem with memory is that most
memories are dull; what happens,
in general, is mostly dull. I remember

how dull my own boyhood was, the long wait
for something to happen nearly always
ending in disappointment—Martha Watson's

summer dresses nearly falling away,
but never really falling away.
But suppose one morning without rain she found

her way to my room, the sun entering
with her and lighting up the window
and the bed, lighting her dress as it became

liquid and fell down her arms. I think that
would be interesting. And her sad,
small breasts and her strong thighs, lighted up,

would be interesting. I think I would find
everything about her visit
tremendously interesting. That's why even

a little of this extravagance is
so necessary, why, in the strange
and unlikely light of such visitations,

the actual nearly always pales into
embarrassment. It's too serious
to want around, too earnest to put up with

for very long; its straight face can
turn laughter bitter in your mouth, choke
the best parts of your past, ruin your life.

EARLY FROST

This morning the world's white face reminds us
that life intends to become serious again.
And the same loud birds that all summer long
annoyed us with their high attitudes and chatter
silently line the gibbet of the fence a little stunned,
chastened enough.

They look as if they're waiting for things
to grow worse, but are watching the house,
as if somewhere in their dim memories
they recall something about this abandoned garden
that could save them.

The neighbor's dog has also learned to wake
without exaggeration. And the neighbor himself
has made it to his car with less noise, starting
the small engine with a kind of reverence. At the window
his wife witnesses this bleak tableau, blinking
her eyes, silent.

I fill the feeders to the top and cart them
to the tree, hurrying back inside
to leave the morning to these ridiculous
birds, who, reminded, find the rough shelters,
bow, and then feed.

ANOTHER SONG

Most mornings I wake up slowly. That's just
the way I am. I wake up slow as I can, listening first
to one thing, then another. The milk bottles chiming

just outside the door, then the milktruck idling in the street.
If I'm lucky, the girl through the wall will be singing
and I'll hear her next, singing while she dresses. Maybe

she's brushing her hair, or tying the ribbon for her stocking
—that would be nice. And out in the hall, some man will
probably kiss Miss Weitz good-bye again—yes, I believe

those are their lowered voices now, and that is his cough.
Others are coming out now, their doors opening and closing so
variously, too many to sort out. Why sort them out? And now

the factory whistle is telling the night shift that enough is
      enough.
Now I hear myself humming along, joining in this little chorus
of good intentions. When everything is ready, I'll go out.

YELLOW

The town is much larger than you recall,
but you can still recognize the poor:
they vote to lose every chance they get, their faces
carry the tattoo of past embarrassments,

they are altogether too careful. This girl,
here in the print dress, pretending to shop
for an extravagance, the too slow way
her hand lingers between the colors along

the rack, her tentative hold on the clasp—
sure signs she knows she has no business here.
Soon enough she'll go home again with nothing
especially new in her hand, but no one

needs to rush things. The afternoon itself
is unhurried, and the lighted air outside
the store has lilacs in it. Her hand finds
a yellow dress. I think she should try it on.

YOU WRECK YOUR CAR

Maybe you'll live, maybe some fluke will have
the emergency crew waiting with their pants on.

It could be they weren't even sleeping, just
playing cards or eating fried chicken inside

the station house, drinking nothing but, say,
coffee, just two or three blocks from your mistake.

It turns out they had been ready, eager
even, to make tracks to your accident. They

live for this. Odds are you'll be light-headed,
too giddy maybe to notice much about

how their hands dance, altogether, above
your wounds, or how they pamper you to the cot,

flatter you against all that you deserve,
and float you to the hospital. Your eyes may

fail now, and that familiar weariness
will coax you into accepting sleep, so you'll

never know how, even as you gesture
toward death, your angels are most alive.

IMPERIAL THEOLOGY

Admit it. The Haida were sons of bitches.
Everyone knew that much. While all the good
tribes minded their own stretches of beach, sifting
tide pools for shellfish, taking turns hauling in
salmon, maybe slapping one another
on the back each time someone had nerve enough
to drag in a whale, the Haida worked
to develop a richer taste, a preference for food
other people labored to produce,
and a taste for the necessary
blood they had to spill to get the food.
Their religion was simple: What is good
for the Haida makes good theology.
Their holy men blessed them, after their fashion,
and gave elaborate thanks to their gods
each time the proud elect harvested
another fishing village with their clubs.

INFIRMITIES

Some mornings, you know you've seen
things like this before.
The kind woman across the street
is lame, and her daughter is lame.

Some defect they've had since birth
is working to dissolve their bones.
The boy three doors down
is blind. And the idiot
girl who sweeps up at the market
insists all day on her own
strange tune. And sometimes they seem
happy enough and sometimes
you might find one alone, muffling
grief with a coat sleeve.

And the shy way the blind boy
laughs when he stumbles
makes you laugh with him some mornings.
Some mornings it hurts to see.

CHORE

Of course, what we actually feel is too much
a grab-bag of longing to be anything so simple

as an emotion. What we actually feel could never
be pinned down to a word. My father

was dying, and I was home for a visit.
I did a few chores to help us all get ready.

To speak of how I felt would be a mistake.
I was splitting firewood, loading the woodbox.

It was hard work, and I found some pleasure in it.
I was at the back corner of my father's house,

a place I hadn't seen in years, working easily
and well, my shirt off in the last heat of summer.

Wiping the sweat from my face, I looked up
and saw him, saw that he had been watching me.

We met as well as we could. Behind him a huge jay
bowed a heavy branch. I pointed to the hysterical bird.

Nothing much happened after that. I swung the axe
until I finished the work.

ANOTHER KISS

Far sweeter as a greeting, this parting
of lips became the concluding gesture
love would bear between my father and me.
In this last hour of his death his fever
had retreated so that as my kiss found
the smooth passage of his neck, I felt
how the cold surprise was beginning there.

And so we waited, and I kept my sight
fixed upon his face, which worked with less
conviction—which appeared to acquiesce.
I studied his preference for fainter effort:
the softening of his brow, the rounding
edges and, as if he could speak, the slight
movement of his lips, nearly opening.

All of this, so I would remember the hour
and the moment of my father's death,
so I might rehearse the silent language
of this final speech. His lungs were filling
and gave him less and less reason to breathe.
Lifting briefly, his lips in the semblance
of a kiss, and a kiss, a third kiss, he was gone.

AFTER THE LAST WORDS

By now I'm dead. Make what you will of that.
But granted you are alive, you will need
to be making something more as well. Prayers
have been made, for instance, but (trust me)

the dead are oblivious to such sessions.
Settle instead for food, nice meals (thick soup):
invite your friends. Make lively conversation
among steaming bowls, lifting heavy spoons.

If there is bread (there really should be bread),
tear it coarsely and hand each guest his share
for intinction in the soup. Something to say?
Say it now. Let the napkins fall and stay.

Kiss each guest when time comes for leaving.
They may be embarrassed, caught without wit
or custom. (See them shifting from foot to
foot at the open door?) Could be you will

repeat your farewells a time or two more
than seems fit. But had you not embraced them
at such common departures prayers will
fall as dry crumbs, nor will they comfort you.

EMBALMING

You'll need a corpse, your own or someone else's.
You'll need a certain distance; the less you care
about your corpse the better. Light should be
unforgiving, so as to lend a literal
aspect to your project. Flesh should be putty;
each hair of the brows, each lash, a pencil mark.

If the skeleton is intact, its shape may
suggest beginnings of a structure, though even here
modification might occur; heavier
tools are waiting in the drawer, as well as wire,
varied lengths and thicknesses of doweling.
Odd hollows may be filled with bundled towel.

As for the fluids, arrange them on the cart
in a pleasing manner. I prefer we speak
of *ointments*. This notion of one's anointing
will help distract you from a simpler story
of your handiwork. Those people in the parlor
made requests, remember? Don't be concerned.

Whatever this was to them, it is all yours now.
The clay of your creation lies before you,
invites your hand. Becoming anxious? That's good.
You should be a little anxious. You're ready.
Hold the knife as you would a quill, hardly at all.
See the first line before you cross it, and draw.

THE END OF THE WORLD

The end of the world occurs with the first thaw. Waking from his first restful night in many months—a night without shivering, without cramping muscles—the last man lifts his head from the straw, hears snow-melt trickling, sees morning light through the window's ice, smells the scent of earth, lies back, and dies because he cannot bear to go through it all again.

But that is a very limited view of the event. The end was more than the final exhaustion of the last man. Actually, some of the most interesting events of human history occurred just prior to this last gesture, which is not surprising if you take into account the fact that, in the last years of human experience, irony flourished.

The last man was a Jew, a fact that he ignored for many years—most of his life, really. But as years passed and he came to realize his status as last man, the fact of his Jewishness became an insider's joke. The first time he laughed in his adult life was related to his Jewishness; he was picking rust from a can of peaches when he remembered *Torah*, the covenant.

But, as you might suspect, there were many years when the last man was not alone, was not, in simple words, the last man, not yet. Twenty years before the end of the world, the last man was married to one of the last women; they even had a son together and for several months entertained hopes of survival. Later, they parted, mostly out of bewilderment.

If you must know, the last man thought he was the last man some time before he actually was. Many miles away, the second-to-last man lived quietly in a shopping mall. He cut his foot on something in the hardware store and died of tetanus. All told, there were about two years when the last man was mistaken, but that had no effect upon perceptions concerning his lastness.

The last man was the last for about five years and three months, though you could argue he was last for seven years and three months, depending. Anyway, one of the more curious outcomes was that he forgot his name. There is no reliable method for determining when, exactly, he forgot his name; by the time he realized he had forgotten his name he'd also forgotten when he last knew it.

Even so, it is safe to say that he was without a name for the better part of his last year. This was the beginning of an astonishing freedom. The last man had always enjoyed books; that was fortunate. Following the loss of his name, and having acquiesced to lastness, the last man became the first reader. He shrugged off identity and became multiple, embracing all.

He became the author of many great works, indestructible works. The loss of his name was the beginning of this translation, and the loss of his name brought about the loss of many other limitations. He looked up from his canned peaches, looked around, saw the end of the world, and felt pretty relaxed.

As an agnostic, the last man had seldom prayed. But as his final days diminished, he began to address God. He also prayed to answer, to respond to his own petitions. As God of the last man, he was compelled to deny every request—the plea for companionship, for understanding, for true wisdom, for a pure heart. He denied the last man everything, but always with good reason.

II.
Leaving Florianopolis

Soon I shall know who I am.

—*Borges, "In Praise of Darkness"*

IN PRAISE OF DARKNESS

Here, behind this attic door is Borges,
waiting in a straight chair, bound there
by thin wire and by rags. Soon you will
ask him the questions again, and soon

he will say his answers, his insane
and foolish words, smiling as if he had said
enough, as if he had answered what you've asked.
And you will hit him again, and split

his skin; you'll invent pain and slowly
let him know what it is you've made.
But, as before, nothing will have changed.
If he speaks at all he'll only say his

nonsense to the air until you must
hit again to make him stop. So you
come to hate the hand that pulls open
the attic door, that gives you Borges,

waiting in a straight chair, looking out
from the corner of an attic room. There is
a wash of light from the window, and it warms
his face, his arms; he feels it pouring

through the neat, dark suit he wears.
You believe he is mad. He is too old
for this and nearly blind, and the light
on his face makes him beautiful.

When you enter the room, he sees
an angel enter; he turns his head
toward your noise, his face expectant.
You have never been so loved.

LUCIFER'S EPISTLE TO THE FALLEN

Lucifer, Son of the Morning, Pretty Boy,
Rose Colored Satan of Your Dreams, Good as Gold,
you know, God of this World, Shadow in the Tree.

Gorgeous like you don't know! Me, Sweet Snake, jeweled
like your momma's throat, her trembling wrist. Tender
as my kiss! Angel of Darkness! Angel

of Light! Listen, you might try telling *me*
your troubles; I promise to do what I can.
Which is plenty. Understand, I can kill

anyone. And if I want, I can pick
a dead man up and make him walk. I can
make him dance. Any dance. Angels don't

get in my way; they know too much.
God, I love theater! But listen, I know
the sorry world He walks you through.

Him! Showboat with the Heavy Thumbs! Pretender
at Creation! Maker of Possibilities!
Please! I know why you keep walking—you're skittish

as sheep, and life isn't easy. Besides,
the truth is bent to keep you dumb to death.
Imagine! The ignorance you're dressed in!

The way you wear it! And His foot tickling
your neck. Don't miss my meaning; I know none
of this is your doing. The game is fixed.

Dishonest, if you ask me. So ask. God
knows how I love you! My Beauty, My Most
Serious Feelings are for you, My Heart turns

upon your happiness, your ultimate
wisdom, the worlds we will share. Me, *Lucifer.*
How can such a word carry fear? *Lucifer,*

like love, like song, a lovely music lifting
to the spinning stars! And you, my cooing
pigeons, my darlings, my tender lambs, come, ask

anything, and it will be added to your
account. Nothing will be beyond us; nothing
dares touch my imagining.

FALSE ANGELS

If they can remember heaven at all,
the memory is a version you would not
recognize: There was some business
about light, a disturbing radiance
flowing from each stern figure in their past.

Often, they have bad dreams, visitations
of endless movement in limitless space,
a gesture which once might have brought
. . . was it elation? which now evokes mere
queasiness, heart's vertigo. The worst?

An unbearable memory of Him:
that turbulence in which they would swim,
appalling embrace, eternal chasm,
that heady balm, passion's flood and fire,
which without understanding they desire.

HOMELAND OF THE FOREIGN TONGUE

Each morning we begin again. My wife
wakes me with a shove, and condescends to try
her sorry Deutsch with me; she's chewing mud.
God, she's dumb. I tell her so, but mostly
in a dialect she never understands.
Carefully now, she mouths her thanks and takes me

by the hand to the dampness of the trough,
where she leaves me throwing water on my face.
I wash those parts I want to wash, begin
my bump along the wall to the sour kitchen,
where coffee waits and something tasteless chills
against the plate. Grace is blind, and probably

deaf as well, happens only where angels
let it—nowhere you'll ever find in time.
I've never seen the woman's face, though once,
too far from here to count for much, I wished I could.
But it's morning come again, and she,
as is her habit, begins to sing above the soup.

Somewhere, some angel pities me, as God
must once have pitied her: Her voice forgets
its tenement, and I neglect the words.

LOST CITIES: CALVINO

Already, the room seems smaller, and I forget which
version of the world I was visiting last. My eyes
have found a way of closing by themselves, and if I sleep,
I feel as if I could sleep forever in my dream.

For a time, at any rate, the way seemed clear enough.
It was as if, if your town were dying, you still had choices,
as if you could die right along with that unhappy place,
or live as you might, somehow beyond its pettiness.
So, I look at myself and I imagine a man I love
lying too quietly across a pallet, barely breathing,
and losing ground while I watch.

In this version, maybe I don't know him well,
but have only come across some things he's done,
things that have made me better, or have made me
think more generously than I might have on my own.
That would be reason enough to love him, I think.
So today I imagine I love him as I love myself.
I wish him well.

When I was a boy, I stepped off a train and had
a beautiful thought: There are places in the world
where people have been dying forever. For instance,
you step out from your train some bright yellow day in April
and there you have it, there beneath your feet—that silent,
crushed city. It occurs to me that I don't have to settle
for that kind of waste, and so I don't.

Tired as I am, I imagine my city alive again. And if I want,
I make it better than it was, and the people better
than they would have been. If you let it, a lie so generous
as this can redeem the whole embarrassment. It's not
a bad way to travel, bumping into remarkable towns
you might have missed, or maybe mourned for. There is
no unnecessary art to this. Just imagine: From his heaven, God

watches all these poor, dim images approaching the invisible
door, again and again, in fear. Could be he pulls his beard
wanting to wake those shadows up to loveliness, to the joy
in making a new world from nothing, or a world
from nearly nothing, a world from the giddy expectations
crowded in a single word.

Then what of those Lost Cities? Of course they can't be
truly lost, only hidden behind some regrettable veil
of grief, maybe dying for the lack of a little humor
to put some color to their faces once again. Against such
possibilities, death has no significance, or not enough.
I think again of the cricket which woke me late last night,
or which woke me once some night long ago, or perhaps

I only imagine a cricket trying to keep itself awake
by singing the only song it has, but giving everything it has
to—is it loveliness? I like to think there must be some deeply
buried artifact compelling something more than style,
more than postures struck. Hearts, for instance, pronouncing
all they hear or think they hear as clearly as they can.

And now this man I never knew well enough is dying,
and dying sings more than I can hold. My worlds increase
without me. They pull me after them. Me, Calvino.
In my solitary bed I'm not alone. God love us, Where
is the lovely book I lent the boy? The boy who had no idea
what it was he held, held weeping for his loneliness and pain.
I couldn't help him, but handed him a book I loved.

Unlike these tormented ones, I cannot live on happenstance.
I am too happy to make a poem from what I know.
Bless me I am deeply tired now. A thousand invisible cities
all demanding my attention. If you love me wish me well.

AN IRONY

Like looking too long into a father's death,
this puzzling affection can require too much.
Then comes the greater trouble, when you begin
to suspect your words—even those that caress
the tongue—point only to other, ever
diminishing words, or only to desires,
vague and untouched by the welcomed response
of flesh, the deeper assurance of live bone.
Few can bear to suspect how little
their conversations have to do with breath.

COMING FORTH

—Lazarus speaks

I'm sorry, I have a hard time not laughing
even now. This ridiculous grin

won't get off my face. Dying did it,
though I don't remember much about

being dead. Sometimes, horrible things happen:
children die, famine sets in, whole towns

are slapped down and turned to dust by earthquake.
I can't help it, but these things start me

laughing so I can't stop. My friends all hate me.
The morning my sister cracked her hip,

I was worthless; I had to run clear out
to the clay field to keep anyone from seeing

how it broke me up. I know. You think
I'm trash, worse than a murderer

or a petty god. I suppose I am.
I just get this quiver started

in me every time someone I know dies and stays dead.
I tremble all over and have to hold

myself, as if some crazy thing in me
were anxious to get out. I told you

I can't remember being dead. I can't.
But this weakness in my knees, or in my throat

keeps me thinking—whatever comes next
should be a thousand worlds better than this.

THE SHERIFF'S LAST PRONOUNCEMENT

Go out there if you want to; I am,
frankly, too weary of this business

to care. But stick around if you don't
mind hearing the truth. I'll only tell

it once. After that, I'm going back
to my books for a little real life.

Your old friend, that Hood, is nothing but
a pimply kid who pockets every

coin he takes. The lout won't even spend,
just likes to watch the gold pile up.

I'm told he even pees on it just
to keep his sorry band of piss ants

from touching any of it. I may as well
tell you now—your sweet Marian

hasn't been a maid since she was eight.
She pees on her gold too. For all I know,

the whole lot of them does nothing but
steal, copulate, and pee. It isn't fear

that keeps me from the forest; the whole
place reeks. Give me Nottingham *any*

day—a man knows what he can touch
and what he can't. Your merry band

can have the whole stinking world and *all*
the gold. I'm not going out again.

ARCHAEOLOGY: THE FIRST LECTURE

But we needn't be troubled with much more
talk of these, except to say that their gods
were bloody, and so *they* were bloody; they
also stank, ate meat, and left their feces
where they fell. Beyond these things, they remain
for the most part unremarkable, not
generous to further study, and sadly dull.

I recall my own disappointment in
their bones—dark, stiff things, just fists and twisted
limbs; crania—fruitless gourds, uninteresting
as dust. Murder, you'll note, continued to be
their most natural cause of death, though
these murders were themselves uninteresting
—typically something blunt cracking a thick skull.

We may as well move to another locale,
unless some question remains concerning
these thugs, or their demise, or the simple
construction of their weapons, which was their
chief religion, it seems, and their only art.
Where such knowledge leads—who would say?
Surrounding debris suggests their bellies were full.

LEAVING FLORIANOPOLIS

Carlos I said to myself, which was so
unlike me because my name is not Carlos,

but *Carlos*, I said, *Never fail to do
what is necessary under heaven.*

Good advice, I thought at the time
and think so still. But, as necessity

was flourishing so remarkably well
upon departure, I had to lie down.

It was then, opening one eye ever
so slightly, I witnessed the deft flex

of anonymous legs approaching.
These were long and slender and of a hue

a painter in oils would call sienna, use
to limn his garden stalks. I closed my eyes

as she whose dark limbs approached leaned close,
her breath like exotic flowers—all of them blue.

Into the cup of my ear she breathed *Eugene*,
or was it *Raymond*, thinking to wake me

for some device in the hammock. I feigned sleep
and so allowed her whatever game she pleased.

She changed my name many times, but for each
small outrage of the tongue her invention

more than compensated. She wore me so,
I had to feign waking to plead sincere

exhaustion. Listening then to what I took
to be her burnt sienna feet, staccato

across the bright tiles, I dreamed once again
of Florianopolis, that untoward port

whose intriguing flues line the coastal curve
in such alluring designs, and whose women

are forever bidding strangers farewell
with lush gestures, their cool habit of approach,

their lips' blue buds parting, their famous kiss.
Oh, Carlos! How can you leave like this?

STILL WAITING

—for Kavafy

Yes, and after all of this we stand, still waiting
for those quaint people to arrive, and to accomplish
their famous work among us. And isn't it just like
barbarians to make us wait. It's been so long since

we first made ready that the town could use another
coat of paint. Someone should probably feed
the children. The senator might as well take his seat.
The feasting tables have begun to stink; servant boys

can't keep the birds away. Without a breath of wind,
the pennants hang like laundry. The afternoon is
failing altogether. Evening, as they say, is already
at the gate. So I embroider this longest part

of an exaggerated day, drawing with a stick
to relieve the wait. I should have known—I'm sure
I told them—these foreigners are always on their way;
they are forever late. Just the same, we know they must

be coming. What else could they do? They have
so little patience, no interest in board games, books,
or conversation. Slow as they are, they could hardly
stay home—so easily bored, so discontent, so great.

THE MUMMY VIEWED

Laid out in delicate repose for visitants
like us, who come dumbly believing we have come
for another of those fifty-cent amusements
and wish we had not come, had left the children home,

there she is: a girl, ancient, perfectly chaste
though stripped of more than clothes, stripped of all
so that even what survives, formally debased,
has suffered an alien and drastic memorial.

And then the puzzlement: given spirit and flesh,
which element has been surrendered, which displaced?
as crowding we peer from ordinary callousness
into the carved Egyptian jasper of her face—

like staring into any neat and bloodless wound
whereof the pain is disproportionate: a paper cut,
those open, emptied hands Christ offered to the room
of Thomases, or this queer, human apricot.

REGARDING THE MONUMENT

But roughly but adequately it can shelter
what is within (which after all
cannot have been intended to be seen).
—Elizabeth Bishop

Of course it is made of *would*, and *want*,
the threads and piecework of *desire*. Its shape
is various, always changing but always
insufficient, soliciting revision.

     I thought you said it was made of *wood*.
     You said it was made of wood.

Never mind what I may have said; I might
have said anything to bring you this close
to the monument. As far as that goes,
parts of it *are* wood, parts are less, more.

     Some kind of puzzle? What can it do?
     If the wind lifts again we're in trouble.

Certain of its features endure—its more
sepulchral qualities—whether it gestures
ahead or back, the monument
is always in some sense memorial.

     Is it safe? It looks so unstable.
     Do you think it's safe to come so close?

I don't think it's safe, but I don't think safe matters.
It's changing. Even now. Watch how it turns
into its new form, taking something
of what it was, taking something else.

       I don't feel well. Does it have to do that?
       Is it growing? Still? Something must be wrong.

The monument is growing still, even if
diminishment must be a frequent stage
of its progress. If we return tomorrow
it may appear much less; it may seem gone.

       I don't see the point. What is the point?
       I'm leaving now; you stay if you want.

But the part that lies buried, its foundation,
will forge its machinery ever and again,
and the wind will return it to motion,
if more powerfully, and more horribly.

III.
The Translation of Raimundo Luz

I show you a mystery: we shall not all sleep,
but we shall all be changed.

—Paul to the Corinthians

Biographical Note

Raimundo Luz is the greatest postmodern poet writing
in Portuguese. He has never left his birthplace,
Florianopolis, Brazil. His father was a mender of fishing
nets, his mother a saloon singer. He has no formal
education, having gathered all he knows from books.
He reads seven modern languages, also ancient Hebrew,
ancient Greek, and Latin. Luz is best known as a radical
theologian, identifying himself paradoxically as a
Christian-Marxist. He is a devoted family man, a fan of
American rhythm and blues, an accomplished cook, and
a fiction.

THE TRANSLATION OF RAIMUNDO LUZ

1. My Infancy

How like a child I was! So small and so
willing! And the world was extravagant,

and beyond reach even then. All those lovely
apparitions flitting close, and then away—

I loved them. Even their inconstancy.
God was always tapping his curious

music in my head. I'm sure I *seemed* aloof,
but the opposite was true—such a pleasant

distraction, so good, this music of God,
his calming voice. Wonderful odors

everywhere—these dark, human odors.
Sometimes I would taste them. And the salt

of mother's breast, yes, and then that sweet milk
of dreams, dreams and appalling distance.

2. My Personal History

Mother bore me without pain.
Something of a miracle I'd say.
Father never doubted my love.
My brother was my better self.
All these frail poems
—beloved sisters.

Good fortune everywhere.
Grace, abundant and wet on our faces.
Exotic fruits plentiful as grass.
God still humming his engaging lyric
in my ear. Air?
Tender, sweet cake.

Just out the door—a jungle.
Just out the door—a blue sea.
And always, between sleep
and waking, between waking
and sleep, this marvelous
confusion of a jungle and a sea.

And later, so many beautiful
women to marry.
They all cared for me.
I married the most generous.

We have a daughter
who resembles me,
but so prettily.
A great miracle.

One morning we three
slept luxuriously in the same bed.
In her drowse, the baby nursed.
God loves Raimundo.
I woke first.

3. My Language

Portuguese is my language,
and that is appropriate.
That is as it should be.

A language somewhat akin
to Spanish, but with ironic
possibilities as well. A perfect
language for my purposes.
One does not weep in Portuguese.

Can you hear its music, its
intelligent distance? (No, of course not.
You are not reading Portuguese now.)

The boats in the harbor are rapt
in conversation with the sea.
The air sings high Portuguese.

When I was a boy, I nearly learned
German too. A narrow escape.
I am careful to avoid things German,
in particular the food. As for English,
I leave that now to whomever needs it.
I never look north from Florianopolis.

Here, I have everything I need: a generous woman,
this daughter, my garden, Portuguese.

4. My Mortal Dream

In which I am driving through what I presume
to be a northamerican city: I have never seen
a northamerican city, but I think this one is St. Louis.
It is not a very clean city, even the air has fingerprints,
windows of the huge tenements are without glass.
The few people I catch sight of are sleepwalking.

At the signal I stop my car, which I believe
is a Volkswagen. I wait for the light and examine
my surroundings. A man with a gun is taking money
from a station attendant. He counts the bills
and shoots the man, who then seems a boy, and now
a sack of leaves. The criminal lifts his face to mine
and I nod. He points. I turn to face the light. The car
window explodes in my ear, and my life begins.

5. My Imitation

I sold my possessions, even the colorful pencils.
I gave all my money to the dull. I gave my poverty
to the president. I became a child again, naked
and relatively innocent. I let the president have my guilt.

I found a virgin and asked her to be my mother.
She held me very sweetly.

I watched father build beautiful shapes with wood.
He too had a gentle way.

I made conversation in holy places with the chosen.
Their theater was grim.

I suggested they cheer up. Many repented,
albeit elaborately.

I floated the wide river on a raft.
I set Jim free.

I revised every word.

One morning, very early, I was taken by brutes and beaten.
I was nailed to a cross so sturdy I thought
father himself might have shaped it.

I gestured for a cool drink and was mocked.
I took on the sins of the world and regretted my extravagance.
I gave up and died. I descended into hell
and spoke briefly with the president.

I rose again, bloodless and feeling pretty good.

I forgave everything.

6. Our Lost Angels

Ages ago, clouds brought them near
     and rain brought them to our lips;
     they swam in every vase, every cupped palm.
     We took them into ourselves
     and were refreshed.
For those luckier generations, angels
     were the sweet, quickening substance
     in all light, all water, every morsel of food.
Until the day the sun changed some, as it had,
     took them skyward, but thereafter
     the clouds failed to restore them.

In time, streams gave up

    every spirit, and the sea, unreplenished,

    finally became the void we had feared

    it would become, the void we had imagined.

And, as now, clouds brought only rain,

    and the emptied rain

    brought only the chill in which

    we must now be wrapped.

7. Embarrassment

The witness caught Raimundo's drift and looked away.
A stale taste dried his open mouth.

The girl in the upper room dressed the ancient doll.
The witness spat, began to pout.

Raimundo shrugs and scribbles on a yellow pad.
The problem's not so simple. Stick around.

8. My Goodness

    I have such good intentions.

    I have enormous sympathy.

    I am aware of a number

    of obligations.

    In the Hebrew, Enoch

    walked with God and was no more.

    A difficult translation,

    but so intriguing!

I am a little skeptical,

but nonetheless intrigued.

How far must one walk

in such cases?

I suppose I shouldn't tell you,

but I have suspected something

like this. I have had an inkling.

Call it a hunch.

Even so, I manage so little faith.

My goodness is deficient.

I walk for days and looking up

bump again into my own door.

9. My Incredulity

Lazarus, of course,

is another story altogether.

Lazarus does not

engage my better self, nor interest me.

Drink twice from the same

wrong cup? Say the idiot boy falls down,

gets back up and falls

again—this is some great trick?

Our giddy crowd should swoon?

Does the first runner turn back to mock the lost?

And if he does, should we

praise him for his extravagant bad taste?

No. His sort will not
profit close attention. His story—

neither lawful nor
expedient. Tear your linens to winding cloth.

Wrap him once for all.
When you've finished with your napkin, bind his lips.

He has had his say.
Bury Lazarus as often as it takes.

10. My Denial

Such a very long night. So demanding
of one's better judgment. I was alone.

Or I seemed alone. My friends had all left
on earlier trains. The raised platform

I paced was poorly lit, my train not due
for another hour. Then the strange man came.

He walked past me once, then turned, surprised;
his appearance—either frightened or insane.

He pronounced a name—certainly foreign—
asked if we hadn't perhaps met before.

If he was familiar, it was nothing
more than a resemblance to any chance

acquaintance. I told him no, he was mistaken.
The wind came up like a howl. He left me.

From behind my book I watched him settle in
at the platform's farthest end. I checked the time,

my train still far away. Then, the soldiers came,
maybe a dozen soldiers. They appeared

suddenly and from every passage.
They came to me rudely, demanded my name.

I told them my business. I was waiting
for a train. Their captain pointed to the stranger

at the platform's end and asked me
if I knew the man. No, I said, I am only

waiting for a train. They ignored me and ran
to the other's bench. They slapped him awake,

picked him up by his coat front and began
dragging him my way. As they pushed past,

I asked what he had done. The captain stopped,
asked why I had to know. Was I his friend?

No, I said, I've never seen him before tonight.
I don't know the man at all. Take him.

11. My Good Luck

Fortunately, there are mitigating circumstances.
Fortunately, Raimundo doesn't get what he deserves.
Confronted by embarrassment, I lift my bed and walk.

The comfort lies in fingering the incoherent for the true.
The comfort lies in suspecting more than evidence allows.
My only rule: If I understand something, it's no mystery.

As you might suppose, I miss my father very much;
and if I think of his dying, I can become deeply sad.
Giving yourself to appearances can do a lot of harm.

So I remember the morning my father died, and the ache
of his relief, the odd, uncanny joy which began then,
and which returns unbidden, undeserved, mercifully.

12. My Amusing Despair

I confess that I am not
a modern man. As a modern man
I am a little flawed.
Raimundo is much too happy.

Many times, more times
than I would care to admit to you,
I have suffered from this
unforgivable lack, this absence.

All around me, poets
tearing at their bright blouses, tearing
at their own bare flesh.
All night long—their tortured singing.

And still I have suffered
an acute lack of despair. Why is that?
Is Raimundo stupid?
Am I unfeeling? Doesn't the bleak

weight of the north ever
pinch my shoulders? Well, no, not often.
And when it does—which is
not very often—I can't help feeling

a little detached. As if
I had somewhere else to go. As if
I were a spectator,
a dayworker watching the slow clock.
I have an interest in the outcome,
but not a strong interest.

13. My Farewell

Things are happening. Daily,
I come across new disturbances
in my routine. I am curiously
unsettled. I dress myself
and the clothes fall to the floor.
I scratch my head. Dust
in my hand. All morning
arranging flowers, and for what?
Petals fallen, litter
on the pretty cloth. I march
straightway to the mirror
and shake my fist. My hand
is a blue maraca scattering petals.
I shout my rage
and hear my words praising
the vast goodness of the world.
This is beyond control.

Even so, I am slowly learning one thing;
of one thing I am slowly becoming
aware: whether or not I would
have it so, whether I sleep
or no, I will be changed.
I am changing as I speak. Bless you all.
Suffer the children. Finished. Keep.

FIGURES FOR THE GHOST

(1994)

for Marcia
and for our children,
Elizabeth and Benjamin

The apparition of God to Moses began in light;
afterwards God spoke to him in a cloud;
and finally in the darkness.

—GREGORY OF NYSSA

INSCRIPTION

After the plague had come and gone a second time,
after the panic, after the convulsive festival,
after the silence had set in a second time,
I was astonished to observe I was still standing.

And there were one or two others in my region
similarly astonished and similarly
alone, but we kept apart, preferred not to tempt
fate—as it were—preferred this monastic enterprise,

which we, I suppose, undertook in a mixture
of mute relief and nagging culpability.
Nor did I presume the serpentine contagion
had withdrawn completely. The last outbreak had laid

a great litter of corpses, some of which yet offered
trembling carrion to what few corruptible
beasts survived with strength enough to forage still.
Along every path, at the edge of every

stubble field, anonymous remains flourished,
tattered like springtime gardens after rain. And one
knew better than to enter any darkened dwelling,
aware of what surely lived there now. I drew

my shelter from the mud and stone far from any road,
any chance for intercourse, and lay me down within,
having resisted just long enough to engrave
my puzzlement, this witness, in a likely rock.

Murmur

THE HOLY GHOST

Don't worry about it. Other figures would serve as well,
so long as they too imply the sort of appalling stasis
which still provokes unseen, albeit suspected, motion:
a murmur caught in the throat, heart's stammer, vertigo.

A windmill! Now that's lucky. But only if the rope is
secure which holds the lead blade to the anchor,
only if, against the fiercest gale, the blades cannot turn,
though they tremble, though they threaten even to come
   crashing

down, or to be torn away, carried—perhaps spinning now
and deadly—to some murderous reunion with the earth.
Well, that's a little theatrical, but you see what I mean.
The issue is the flight one's mind provides while influenced

by that shuddering stillness making itself . . . what? Supposed?
There were so many distractions along that narrow bay,
so many nearly invisible coves you would not find
unless your boat was slow enough let you trace the seam.

My fortune was the little coracle I had occasion
to row across the inlet. In retrospect, the chore
appears habitual, as if whole seasons had been measured
by my pulling against my grip on the chirping oars,

watching my wake's dissolution, its twin arms opening
to a retreating shore. And, true enough, I may have crossed
that rolling gulf many times each day in fair weather. Still,
I suspect this part I remember best happened only once:

I am rowing steadily enough, davening across
that bay and reaching the choppy center where I pause,
ostensibly to rest. But the breeze also stops, and a calm
settles upon those waters so suddenly I worry

for my breath, and can hardly take it in. And I am struck
by a fear so complete it seems a pleasure,
and I know if I were to look about—though I know better
than to try—I would find the circle of shoreline gone,

and myself adrift in an expanse of stillest waters.
Well, it didn't last. A little air got in, and I sucked it up,
and the boat lifted, almost rocking, across a passing swell.
The shoreline was called back to its place, its familiar shape,

and there were people on it, and I think a couple dogs.
So I kept rowing, though I wouldn't remember until
I'd docked the boat why I'd made the trip. It was an errand
to call my brother back from swimming, which I did.

RETURN DIRECTIVE

Back out of all this now too much for us . . .

The road there—if you take the road and not
the shorter, crude diagonal that cuts
across a ruined and trampled pastureland—
is nearly winding as a spiral stair.

Wind there neither flags nor any longer
rages as a fabled wind might have done;
the winding road grants progressive, hidden
groves where you might find standing still

a profitable diversion from what
journey you thought to take, and each of these
may disclose a path or two—game trails,
but I think more than game might find some use

in taking one. Such a path I'm guessing
may never bring you back, but will demand
another turn, in turn, another choice,
and you will choose and walk, choose and pause.

If lost at all you're lost to those behind you;
to what's ahead you're a kind of imminence.
Besides, whatever loss or gain others
measure, you will know what line you travel

and, if you live and move, how far, how well you fare.

PROSPECT OF THE INTERIOR

A little daunting, these periodic
incursions into what is, after all,
merely suspected territory.

One can determine nothing from the low
and, I'm afraid, compromised perspective
of the ship, save that the greenery is thick,

and that the shoreline is, in the insufficient
light of morning and evening, frequently
obscured by an unsettling layer of mist.

If there are inhabitants, they've chosen
not to show themselves. Either they fear us,
or they prefer ambush to open threat.

We'd not approach the interior at all
except for recurrent, nagging doubts
about the seaworthiness of our craft.

So, as a matter of course, necessity
mothers us into taking stock of our
provisions, setting out in trembling parties

of one, trusting the current, the leaky
coracle, the allocated oar.

THE GLASS MAN

He is the transparence of the place in which He is . . .

This is where he washed to shore
during rough weather in November.
We found him in a nest of kelp,

salt bladders, other sea wrack—
all but invisible through
that lavish debris—and we might

have passed him by altogether
had he not held so perfectly
still, composed, so incoherently

fixed among the general
blowziness of the pile.
Unlikely is what he was,

what he remains—brilliant,
immutable, and of speech
quite incapable, if revealing

nonetheless. Under his foot,
the landscape grows acute, so that it seems
to tremble, thereafter to dissolve,

thereafter to deliver to the witness
a suspicion of the roiling
confusion which brought him here.

SERENADE

The Past? I held it only briefly, but it was mine.
Evenings with The Past were best of all: so much
of the day behind us,

so little left, she would undress by candlelight
(we all had candles then; I'm talking about The Past),
and she was pleased to stand

a long while before me—too long, really—accepting
my eye and the warm swelling of the room, savoring
the wonder of her flesh,

its momentary, astonishing colors pulsing.
Then, the bedclothes, the ribbon at her thigh, the fire
of each trembling candle,

the murmuring of what seemed music in my throat—
all wavering as she like a wave opened
over me and we met.

That was the gift of The Past to me, earlier
version—less elaborate, less mediated
life—but a version without

which I could not be: fragrant oil of The Past, ache
and arc of a reflected radiance, umber
flame coloring our selves.

THE DEATH OF PENELOPE

She went, as you would guess, in her famous,
perversely faithful bed, alone, longing
for her lost boy (wandering desperately
God knows where) her absent daughter (hostage
to a grieving, all-but-luckless suitor,
a petty, hostile man, by all accounts,
incapable of gratitude for what
little luck he onetime must have held)
and longing, if only a little less,
for the hero, long estranged and never
heard from after parting for "one last journey"
to plant an oar in some flat wilderness.
One supposes the clever man must have run
clean through his gamut of tricks, and run out
of stories too, perhaps, as he lay face
down in a stony, treeless field, far from home,
his vast holdings, but approaching the deep,

unpleasant laughter of the inside,
oracular joke, witnessing the dissolve
of all topography, finding against
his face the grinning abyss, himself
unable to let go the little oar.

But as the woman lay dying, for whom
the many-passaged myth was always her
own story, as she lay tasting this new,
sudden pain, which took each harshest, prior
trial and made each a mere cordial
leading to this full draught of bitterness,
just as she glanced about, about to find
herself finally overrun with sorrows,
she found across the room's pure air her loom,
emptied of work, bright with erasure,
bearing only the nothing that suggests,
in its blank face, an approaching visage,
in its stillness, a note rising, as she
fully consumed by pain also rises,
imagines she stares back reading her long
tale of vacancies, pattern of absence,
and constructs of these a new, a stranger
story, now commencing. As the faithless
body and its weakness for toleration
fall finally to the misshapen tree,
Penelope rises, lets fall her dress,
begins the journey, nothing in her hands.

HEROD

The murder of sons? Egyptian motif,
a taste I acquired with the throne—
expedient in the extreme.
Naturally, I began with my own:

Two sons, left alone, become two kings.
Could you expect me to leave them alone?
I've learned what lasts if I've learned at all.
Dead sons, granted, but with a note of renown.

As for my mother? And my wife? Harmless?
Such wombs make kings, save in the tomb.
Shall we say I helped them be harmless?
These chambers are cold; I keep warm.

Regrettable measures, perhaps, but taken;
all of which has left me quite alone.
Hence the two hundred—all of them sons,
bound by the sword to batten down

this monument, to lend a more enduring
radiance, even now, to my pyre.
See how its heat consumes each century,
how these embers dance—music of my fire—

and tender a fair host of mourners
into the bargain. So, the removal of sons
and of the threat of sons? One way to honor
the otherwise forgettable, all my own.

And when Israel is dust, when the weather
of ages erodes the holy in their bins,
I daresay you will remember, with these,
forever my offering to the innocents.

ADVENT

Well, it *was* beginning to look a lot like Christmas—everywhere, children eyeing the bright lights and colorful goods, traffic a good deal worse than usual, and most adults in view looking a little puzzled, blinking their eyes against the assault of stammering bulbs and public displays of goodwill. We were *all* embarrassed, frankly—the haves *and* the have-nots—all of us aware something had gone far wrong with an entire season, something had eluded us. And, well, it was strenuous, trying to recall what it was that had charmed us so, back when we were much smaller and more oblivious than not concerning the weather, mass marketing, the insufficiently hidden faces behind those white beards and other jolly gear. And there was something else: a general diminishment whose symptoms included the Xs in Xmas, shortened tempers, and the aggressive abandon with which most celebrants seemed to push their shiny cars about. All of this seemed to accumulate like wet snow, or like the fog with which our habitual inversion tried to choke us, or to blank us out altogether, so that, of a given night, all that appeared over the mess we had made of the season was what might be described as a nearly obscured radiance, just visible through the gauze, either the moon disguised by a winter veil, or some lost star—isolated, distant, sadly dismissing of us, and of all our expertly managed scene.

CITY UNDER CONSTRUCTION

As you might suppose, the work was endless. Even when at last the City stood gleaming like flame in the troubled radiance of that distended sun, we could not help but be drawn to where our next project should begin: The loosening bolt, flaking surfaces, another unnerving vibration in the yawning superstructure.

We made a joke of it: The Eternal City! And let our lives run out reworking the old failures, refining our materials, updating techniques, but always playing *catch-up* to a construction that just wouldn't hold, fretwork that wouldn't stay put, girders complaining under the accumulating matter of successive generations and an unrelenting wind.

Granted, it could have been worse; at least the work served as an emblem of perpetual promise as every flagging strut commenced another stretch of unquestioned purpose—mornings when we rose from our beds eager and awake, thoroughly enjoyed our food, and hurried out to work.

Nor would it serve to slight the rich pathos we shared like a warming drink with co-workers. For there we'd be—touching up the paint or turning that heavy wrench for the hundredth time—and we'd smile, shake our heads theatrically, say to each other how our City was insatiable.

Just the same, this was not precisely what we had intended—that our City should grow into a self-perpetuating chore. Earlier, we had imagined—more or less naively—a different sort of progress, one with a splendid outcome. We fancied a final . . . *conclusion*, from which we would not be inclined to retreat.

I recall how, long before we had so much as made a start, before we had cleared the first acre or drawn the first plan, we saw the City, and as near completion then as it would ever be, infinite in the best sense, its airy stone reaching to the very horizon, and—I think this is the issue—extending invisibly past.

THE LIE OF THE FUTURE

Some fictions are so pretty you may need to work
an entire lifetime to make up any ground at all,
any real progress against the good intentions
of mad inventors. *The Future*, for one—

tough little brick of a lie, imaginary
road paved with stolen pieces of our puzzlement:
the glib calendar and its rows of blank boxes,
unlikely schemes of lovers, mortgages.

They suggest the dim speculations of the blind,
slender constructions something like the pretty charts
Spanish explorers might have fashioned from thin air.
Except that the world, in this case, *is* flat.

Advance men have peopled it already, arranged
its militant forces and its architecture.
They've established its currency, levied taxes,
left you the bill, already overdue.

And still, *The Future* remains the one eternal
uncreated. It's not waiting, I think. It's just not.

THE HISTORY OF MY LATE PROGRESS

First, what you might call the odd shoe dropping:
the mid-life (well, not—it turns out—*mid*-life)
heart attack, not massive by clinical
standards, but a close call what with fumbling
technicians, a rough ride to emergency.
I thought I was a goner.

> Not really.

No one, I guess, ever really thinks that.
The closest we come is this uncanny,
dispassionate sitting-back, just watching
to see how we'll be saved. And then I was.
It was hard work for all of us, and hard
work for me thereafter,

> tasting the new

bitterness—that any of this could end.
My somatic recovery advanced
passably. I agreed to medication,
certain and acceptable restrictions:
diet, activity, and so on.
I agreed to continue

> as if I'd gained

new enthusiasm for simple things
like fishing, breathing, looking around.
Still, I'd been struck—apparently mid-stride—
by a little surprise. As *that* chagrin
faded, as the dose of bitterness sank
from memory,

> I recalled something else.

Dying (even if I hadn't died, I'd
been dying) had an unexpected slant.
I mean, granted, I had watched those doctors,
their technicians, caught up, extravagant
in their procedures—each of them of *huge*
interest—

         but I was interesting too.
Oddly unafraid. Troubled, but eager.
It is my eagerness *then* which troubles
me now, the exotic thought that I was
more than just willing to see what would come.
Still, recovery is never complete,
which is just as well.

            And in recent years—
the interim—other developments:
diabetes, The Big C (here, then there),
heart surgery. Each brought its own, extreme
demands, new chores, graceless dispensations.
Finally, one's late sentiments catch up
to what the body has

            long determined.
Time. Time out. There has been labor here; one
prefers to imagine there is a style
of progress even after . . . after here.
So, with the merest supposition, I
proposed to recover something I had
lost, had relinquished,

           now just suspected,
and in my so far severed circumstances
found agreeable, vast, beckoning.

THE BEGINNING OF THE WORLD

In the midst of His long and silent observation of eternal presence, during which He, now and again, finds His own attention spiraling in the abysmal soup, God draws up what He will call His voice from unfathomable slumber where it lay in that great, sepulchral Throat and out from Him, in what would thereafter be witnessed as a gesture of pouring, falls the Word, as a bright, translucent gem among primal turbulence, still spinning. Think this is evening? Well, that was night. And born into that turmoil so bright or so dark as to render all points moot, God's pronouncement and first measure.

But before even that original issue, first utterance of our great Solitary, His self-demarcation of Himself, before even that first birth I suspect an inclination. In God's center, something of a murmur, pre-verbal, pre-phenomenal, perhaps nothing more disturbing to the moment than a silent clearing of the hollowed throat, an approach merely, but it was a beginning earlier than the one we had supposed, and a willingness for something standing out apart from Him, if nonetheless His own.

Still, by the time anything so weakly theatrical as that has occurred, already so many invisible preparations: God's general availability, His brooding peckishness, an appetite and predilection—even before invention—to invent, to give vent, an all but unsuspected longing for desire followed by the eventual arrival of desire's deep hum, its thrumming escalation and upward flight into the dome's aperture, already open and voluble and without warning giving voice.

But how long, and without benefit of time's secretarial skills, had that Visage lain facing this direction? What hunger must have built before the first repast? And, one might well ask, to what end, if any? And if any end, why begin? (The imagination's tedious mimesis of the sea.) In the incommensurate cathedral of Himself, what stillness!

What extreme expression could prevail against such self-same weight? And would such, then, be approximate to trinity? An organization, say, like this: The Enormity, Its Aspirations, Its Voice. Forever God and the mind of God in wordless discourse until that first polarity divests a cry against the void. Perhaps it is that first resounding measure which lays foundation for every flowing utterance to come. It would appear to us, I suppose, as a chaos of waters—and everything since proceeding from the merest drop of it.

So long as we have come this far, we may as well proceed onto God's initial venture implicating . . . us, His first concession at that locus out of time when He obtains the absence of Himself, which first retraction avails for all the cosmos and for us. In the very midst of His unending wholeness He withdraws, and a portion of what He was He abdicates. We may suppose our entire aberration to proceed from that dislocated hand, and may suppose the terror we suspect—and which lingers if only to discourage too long an entertainment—to be the trace and resonance of that self-inflicted wound.

So why the vertiginous kiss of waters? Why the pouring chaos at our beginning which charges all that scene with . . . would you call it *rapture*? Perhaps the dawning impulse of our creation, meager as it may have been, pronounced in terms we never heard God's return.

MURMUR

God Stammers with Us . . .
    —*Calvin*

What is this familiar pulse beginning
in the throat which promises to pronounce
for once the heart's severer expectations,
but which will not be articulated
from the glib, unhelpful mass of the tongue?

Late winter, the chill can go either way—
brief renewal, habitual decay.
Against our shore the sea extends again
its unrelenting question, and withdraws.
In such weather, the little boats stay put.

And who can blame them? This uncertainty
is the constant weather our horizon
employs to keep our expeditions brief
and—to the point—ineffectual,
while all the while the cliffs beneath us fail.

Still, the murmur of what the heart would like
finally to say, and so attain, repeats
our trouble: these little ventures with the tongue
are doomed by their very mode of travel.
The limits become what we cannot bear.

DEAD SEA BATHERS

What stillness their hearts must know, these bathers
laid out and glistening along the dissolve
of an ancient sea,

their bodies—so late from brief exercise,
so lately thrown down in exhaustion—
already marbled

with a fine white dust as they stretch across
straw pallets arranged by unseen servants
who, one supposes,

must see what we see. And how calm their thoughts,
these still brilliant shapes, as the mind's ebbing,
the heart's slow measure

lull the vessel and its oils, which now retard
to an all but breathless pace akin
to idiocy,

if saved from just that by the hum of faint
discomfort, that murmur beginning deep
as the flesh is fired.

Disciplinary Treatises

DISCIPLINARY TREATISES

1. On the Holy Spirit

If, upon taking up this or any scripture,
or upon lifting your one good eye to inspect
the faintly green expanse of field already
putting forth its late winter gauze of grasses,

you come to suspect a hushed conversation
under way, you may also find sufficient grounds
to suspect that difficult disposition
we call the Ghost, river or thread drawn through us,

which, rippled as any taut rope might be, lifts
or drops us as if riding a wave, and which fends
off, for brief duration, our dense encumberment
—this flesh and its confusions—if not completely,

if only enough that the burden be felt, just
shy of crushing us.

2. The Embarrassment of Last Things

Already you smile, drop your eyes, and chew your cheek.
Centuries of dire prophecy have taught us all
to be, well, unconvinced. And there have been decades,
entire scores of years when, to be frank, wholesale

destruction didn't sound so bad, considering.
You remember; we were *all* disappointed.
That the world never ended meant we had to get
out of bed after all, swallow another dose

of stale breath with our coffee, scrape the grim ice
from our windshields one more time. On the way to work,
stuck in endless traffic, the radio or some
incredibly sincere billboard would promise us again

an end to this, and for a moment we almost
see it. But we know it's not an end, not really;
it's harder than that—some kind of strenuous chore
stretching out ahead like these stalled cars, showing our

general direction, inadvertently or not mocking our pace.

3. Sacraments

Doubtless, Grace is involved—when is it not?—but its
locus is uncertain, remains the cardinal
catch whenever we dare interrogate again
our sacramental dogma. After all, Grace may

lie, contracted, inaccessible in Yahweh's
ancient vault; and it could be these painstakingly
enacted tokens of mystery are really
about as good as paper money. But what if

even the troubled air we breathe were drenched above
our knowing with the golden balm of Adonai?
Well, I like to get carried away. Never mind
the wearied questions of which and how many dear

rituals may qualify; the dire attributes
of divine participation are what these days
could stand some specifics, or, say, a little more
dogmatic elucidation. For it may be

some dreadful portion—very God of very God—
makes periodic and discreet returns, piecemeal,
sabbatical visitation to a matter
and a territory absenced to suffer

our mutual and—let's face it—flagging venture.
But who knows? The Holy may flourish any form
figuring the self's diminishment,
any conjunctive ebbing which yields a reply.

4. The Communion of the Body

The Christ in his own heart is weaker
than the Christ in the word of his brother.
—Dietrich Bonhoeffer

Scattered, petulant, argumentative,
the diverse members generally find
little, nothing of their own, to offer

one another. Like all of us, the saved
need saving mostly from themselves and so
they make progress, if at all, by dying

to what they can, acquiescing to this
new pressure, new wind, new breath which would fill
them with something better than their own good

intentions. Or schemes of community.
Or their few articulate innovations
in dogma. What the Ghost expects of them

is a purer than customary will
to speak together, a mere willingness
to hear expressed in the fragmentary

figures of one another's speech the mute
and palpable identity they share,
scoured clear of impediment and glare,

the uncanny evidence that here
in the stillest air between them the one
we call the Ghost insinuates his care

for the unexpected word now fondling
the tongue, now falling here, incredible
confession—that they would be believers,

who startle to suspect among the scraps
of Babel's gritty artifacts one stone,
irreducible fossil, capable

of bearing love's unprovoked inscription
in the locus of its term.

5. Angels

As with wine, one might tender an entire lifetime
with hierarchies and their array of habits,

characteristic chores, nearness to the Holy,
their special tricks. One might speculate their number.

And what has *not* been said about these our brothers?
So little of it reliable, so little

corresponding to the actual, to the pure
indifference with which most angels skim aloft

our understanding, either incapable
of seeing our distress, or not interested.

Still, stories—*never* verifiable—persist:
the fortunate warning, the inexplicable swerve.

These insinuate themselves against our better
judgment, provide comfort beyond apparent cause.

There are other stories, after all, more somber
accounts of angelic intercourse: How, by force

or guile, a woman or boy has been taken, made
an unwilling portal for some monstrosity

or one of many lies. This version I believe.
Angels are of two sorts; best not to provoke either.

6. Satan

And while we're on the subject of angels—
their dubious character, their famous
unreliability—we should pause

to examine the notorious, one-
time hero and major disappointment:
The Bright One, chief ingrate to the most high,

morning star, petty prince, *et cetera*.
Say what you dare, he still is somebody.
And, if ever I could open my eyes

sufficiently to see what the air is

full of, I might be torn by his glory

even now, even as it is: rebuked,

diminished, scoured raw unto an extreme

radiance, and I daresay I'd find my

knees, and cower there, and worship him, which

action would gain me a measure of his part.

7. Baptism

Of those first waters in which we rolled and swam oblivious
and from which we fled into this confusion of life and death,
here is a little picture. Granted the scheme has undergone some
modest accommodation for the sake of decorum, practicality,
and—who knows?—our unwillingness to risk a chill, so that
the symbolic return to Christ's dire tableau is, well, less than
obvious, and one might subsequently risk infusing the elements
themselves with a little magic. No real harm there, probably,
unless one is then disinclined to appreciate a metaphor when
it's poured in his face.

In the older way, then, the trembling primitive would be led
into a river where he would likely hear some familiar business
about his being buried, whereupon he would go under. What
each receives at this point—underwater—is fairly individual,
pretty various, unlikely to be written down. But then he is
returned and, surfacing, hears that he is raised in the likeness
of a resurrection. He swims in such affusions as he regains the
littered shore.

8. Blood Atonement

This much we might say with some assurance:
a crucifixion occurred, apparently
gratuitous, but a harsh intersection—

tree and flesh and some iron. We might add
sufficient blood resulted to bring about
a death, the nature of which we still puzzle.

As to why? Why the blood? Why the puzzle?
It seems that no one who knows is saying,
which is not to say we lack opinion.

For while we suffer no shortage of dire
speculation, hardly any of it
has given us anything like a clue.

All we dare is that it was necessary,
that we have somehow become both culprit
and beneficiary, and that we

are left to something quite like a response
to that still lost blood, to the blameless world.

9. Grace

Long before you knew desire, Desire turned
to you, saw you as you are even now—
unlovely, a little embarrassed, dead.

Can you remember the throat's pure pulse first
waking you up to a longing you would
neither fix to a name, nor satisfy?

Probably not. But it must have happened.
For thereafter under the influence
of Desire's instruction, you made desire

the new light by which you would dare proceed,
and it has led you here, where you adopt
the drape of love's body and find your own.

10. A Recuperation of Sin

I suppose we might do away with words like *sin*.
They are at least archaic, not to mention rude,
and late generations have been pretty well schooled

against the presumption of holding *anything*
to be absolutely so, universally
applicable, especially anything like

sin which is, to put it more neatly, unpleasant,
not the sort of thing one brings up. Besides, so much
of what ignorance may have once attributed

to *sin* has been more justly shown to be the end
result of bad information, genetic flaw,
or, most often, an honest misunderstanding.

And I suppose *sin's* old usefulness may have paled
somewhat through many centuries of overuse
by corrupt clergy pointing fingers, by faithless

men and women who have longed more than anything
for a more rigid tyranny over their wives
and husbands, over their somnambulant children.

In fact, we could probably forget the idea
of sin altogether if it were not for those
periodic eruptions one is quite likely

to picture in the papers, or on the TV—
troubling episodes in which, inexplicably,
some giddy power rises up to occasion

once more the spectacle of the innocent's blood.

11. Pain

No new attempt at apology here:
All suffer, though few suffer anything
like what they deserve.

Still, there are the famous *un*deserving
whose pain astonishes even the most
unflinching disciples,

whose own days have been consumed by hopeless
explanation for that innocent whose torn
face or weeping burns

or ravenous disease says simply *no,*
not good enough. This is where we must begin:
Incommensurate

pain, nothing you can hope to finger
into exposition, nothing you can
cover up. A fault

—unacceptable and broad as life—gapes
at your feet, and the thin soil you stand
upon is giving way.

12. The End of Heaven and the End of Hell

At long last the feeble fretwork tumbles
apart forever and you stand alone,
unprotected, undeceived, in fullness.
And we are all there as well, equally

alone and equally full of . . . Ourselves.
Yes, I believe Ourselves is what we then
become, though what *that* is must surprise
each trembling figure; and in horror

or elation the effect will be the same
humility, one of two discrete sorts,
perhaps, but genuine humility.
And that long record of our choices—your

every choice—is itself the final
body, the eternal dress. And, of course,
there extends before us finally a measure
we can recognize. We see His Face

and see ourselves, and flee. And shame—old
familiar—will sustain that flight unchecked,
or the Ghost, forgotten just now—merest
spark at the center—will flare, bid us turn

and flame unto a last consuming light:
His light, our light, caught at last together
as a single brilliance, extravagant,
compounding awful glories as we burn.

Late Epistle

FROM THE FATHER

—qui ex Patre

As you might expect, my momentary vision barely
qualifies: you know, sensation something like the merest
swoon, some uncertainty about why all of a sudden
the back garden, its bamboo and rose, the reaching pecans
(one's apparent field contracting to a field of vision)
took to trembling, as well as other accompanying
uncanniness. I mean, *was* the garden trembling or had
it suddenly, unnaturally stopped? Was the disturbing
motion something I was seeing or something I was
seeing with? And why am I asking you?

Perhaps I'm not. Probably, the most I'm doing is one
kind of homage to a moment and a form, a rhetoric
disclaiming what the habitual senses can't make much of.
This is what I can vouch for: I was at rest in a still,
restful corner of our back garden. I had expected
even to doze, but instead found my attention fixing
all the more alertly on the narrow scene, and then I
wasn't seeing anything at all, which is why I'm less
than eager to call this business exactly a vision.
Does one ever *sink* into a vision?

Let's suppose one might. Once interred, what does one come
      to find?
I found the semblance of a swoon, and began to suspect
ongoing trouble at the heart, a fullness in the throat,
an expanding, treble note whose voice was neither mine alone
nor completely separate. I know enough to know you
cannot believe this, not if I were carelessly intent
on saying it was so. It was a fiction which I chanced
upon as evening overtook our walled back garden—
whether by virtue of light's ebbing or the fortunate
influx of approaching shade, who would say?

LATE EPISTLE

Do thy diligence to return before winter.

Timotheus, late disciple of Christ,
bishop to a burlesque we call the church
at Ephesus, priest, sometime son of Paul.

To that Apostle, whose unsurprising
exhortations and rebukes have arrived
anew—this time imparted by the hand

of Tychicus, old sycophant and drudge.
Grace and peace and whatever else you'll have
from me, and from Him who accepts so much.

I, too, thank God—whom I serve, and without
coaxing—to hear you are well, if somewhat
inconvenienced by this latest Roman

holiday. Nero remains uncertain
as to what to make of you? Rest assured
he will think of something, and when he does

you will be reprieved of our annoying
insufficiency, and—let us be frank—
rid of the fear that we may get it wrong,

that we may take our liberties in Christ
too liberally—all the way to joy.
Yes, I am baiting you, but not to strife,

rather to a manner of repose you
might adopt as you would a broadcloth robe,
one with a little space for the body's

diversities each to entertain
a little breathing room. Yes, I suppose
I have learned a thing or two, most of which

I have gathered from your imprisoned self.
Let me teach these back to you, confident
you have the time to listen, unless our

Nero has become a far braver man
overnight, which is, I'd say, unlikely.
He'd sooner miss a meal than make a god

of Paul. So now, knowing your suffering,
knowing how even your celebrated
wits are tried by the saints' abandonment,

I risk pressing them further. Still, you might
recall *I* have never abandoned you.
So, in mock frustration, your ingrate son

presumes to counsel his venerable—
if lately a little vulnerable—
father. I suggest another likely

possibility regarding how we
belated, disorderly believers
fare at Ephesus: We are suspicious,

frankly, of the certainty you expect
to find among us. Of a morning, we
might arise and stand before our houses,

inclined to discover—as you seem to
discover—in the very road, or in
the field beyond the road, or in the curve

of the horizon some quieting calm
or promise. Instead, in those wavering
figures we recognize a general

solicitude which echoes the troubling,
irrepressible tremor of our thoughts.
As latecomers to the invisible,

we live within our doubt; one might say we
live *by* it, a custom you no longer
entertain, having witnessed your own doubt

snatched from your eyes along with a short-lived,
corrective blindness. So, as one forgoes
a little blindness, one may receive some,

perhaps, in turn. Let me become your eyes
in doubt, just as you have been mine in faith.
Unlike you—and the dwindling apostles

who claim to have seen him, touched him, to have
heard his very voice, witnessed thereafter
the death—we suffer a complicated

circumstance: the moment of such presence
has passed. At each remove—by now these are
countless—another occasion for error

avails another disruption of one's
faith in the integrity of the tale,
another opportunity for pure

elaboration, accidental lapse,
for deliberate (forgive me) deceit.
It is not enough that we dare trust God,

or trust the Christ—we must put faith in what
moves others, men and women like ourselves,
and like ourselves untrustworthy, confused,

given to wishful thinking. Moreover,
I propose it is not fear, exactly,
which compels me and which draws the saints

at Ephesus to the manner of care
we take in laying our testimony
before the lost—not, in any case, fear

of the mundane complexion you imply.
We are not ashamed of Him, not so much
as we've appeared, from time to time, of you.

We hold our faith as boldly as we can—
which is to say, we do not hold it well,
but must rely upon the palpable

reciprocity of the hidden Ghost,
an embarrassment one must take care
not to trifle with, which none would announce

to the mob—the thick and unrepentant
thugs with which our great city populates
its marketplace. Paul, they'd stone you here again,

which would give you Paradise, but earn them
something less—harder heads, deeper blindness,
but not trouble even for a moment

their acquiescence to the apparent
slop jars of their lives. So, at Ephesus
the timid saints proceed as if the blind

might one day be restored to a measure
of sight, at least to the obscurity
which will no longer satisfy itself

that *anything* is clearly seen. Call it doubt
that calls us from the dust at Ephesus,
that bids us walk, and speak, and listen all

the more intently to the words which we
exchange, wanting to hear within our own
surprising utterances the living

pulse we know as the only sound we dare
believe. Forgive us, Paul, if we cannot
quite imitate the figure of yourself.

Remember us once the darkened glass
dissolves, no longer clouds the clarity
of an object seen, of a spoken word.

In the meantime, what have we to do
but doubt the simple reductions of brutes,
savor the trembling aspects of ourselves.

MORTUARY ART

Even the ancient, open gate—whose hinges may
as well be stone, whose purpose has always been
purely ornamental—rests extravagantly
at its protected terminus: black *fleurs-de-lys*
topping a Byzantine blaze of black ironwork.

Once inside, the live-oak- and ash-dappled expanse
of gaudy statuary seems infinite, spreads
far as you can see and, presumably, farther:
a great many winged forms, more or less angelic,
some bearing human burdens, others extending

arms in an open embrace, but all with the same
expressionless faces of weary dockworkers.
Whichever narrow lane you choose, you find ahead
a multitude of crosses: Latin mostly, but
mingled with scores of Greek and Celtic, one or two

Pattée, Botonée, and down a lonely detour
the still, dire flames of one startling, spiny Maltese.
Pausing before any one of these explains
what time is for: lending weather its circumstance
for dissolving whatever it happens across.

All cemetery roads converge upon a center
where—dwarfed and nearly obscured by outsized,
marble masonry and a high ring of ancient
trees (so much like stone)—lies a brackish pool like tar.
Nothing lives in it: its waters compose a grim

accumulation of poisons laid out to keep
the foreground neat, deceptively green, natural.
Still, one is very likely to neglect the font
(so easy it's become to slight what isn't blemished),
and wander off, though the dust of the throat goes drier.

From the shallows of that ruined pool, a copper tube
—flanged at the lip, and no thicker than your finger—
blossoms out beyond its stem into something
of a calyx, or white anemone, a wavering
rush of water so pure you'll want to drink of it.

One imagines we need not confuse the fountain
with its pool any more than we need pretend
the gate, the angels, the scores of crosses partake
in our little stroll among the dead, or suffer
interest in our being here among them.

In that cove, water from the font leaps up, its foam
drawing light from some obscurity beyond the trees,
inviting all who have come this far to proceed
a little farther, to press their lips against
the rising pulse where all may drink or may withdraw.

RECOVERED BODY

(1998)

for my brother

Love Him in the World of the Flesh;
And at your marriage all its occasions shall dance for joy.
—W. H. AUDEN, FROM "FOR THE TIME BEING"

NECROPOLITAN

Not your ordinary ice cream, though the glaze
of these skeletal figures affects
the disposition of those grinning candies
one finds in Mexico, say, at the start of November,
though here, each face is troublingly familiar,
exhibits the style adopted just as one declines
any further style—nectar one sips just as he
draws his last, dispassionate breath, becomes
citizen of a less earnest electorate. One learns
in that city finally how to enjoy a confection,
even if a genuine taste for this circumstance
has yet to be acquired, even if it is oneself
whose sugars and oils now avail a composure
which promises never to end, nor to alter.

I.
Deep Below Our Violences

ALEXANDRIAN FRAGMENTS

after the fire

In those uncertain hours following our famous
conflagration, I surveyed with no small measure
of chagrin the scorched rubble, the thousand thousand

scroll rods charred and emptied of all but ashen curls,
steaming parchment, the air bitter and far too hot,
our book vaults fallen, the books reduced to cinder.

And in that moment the sun first lit our city's
eastern quarter, I found myself alone, in awe:
from that ruin, a forest had sprung up overnight,

as a wavering expanse of smoke white trees, pale
birches, original as the local laurel,
but shifting with the morning's faintest breath. They rose

to where their reaching branches twined to canopy
our broad destruction, so that each trunk expanded
at its uppermost and wove a fabric overhead—

now white, now red, now golden from the sun's approach.
Beneath that winding sheet our ravished corpus lay
razed, erased, an open, emptied volume in repose

insisting either new and strenuous reply,
or that we confess our hopelessness and turn away.

ARCHAEOLOGY: A SUBSEQUENT LECTURE

You're thinking that the present site favors
a broad expanse of fallow farmland more
than it does a fallen city. Let that be Lesson One.

The city is there, and none too deep. Soon
as we begin, you'll be surprised how thin
the veil turns out to be. You'll be surprised

how much survives interment, how little
survives intact. For the most part, our city
comes out in pieces, puzzling as any

deliberately jigsawed for an evening's
entertainment. And as you might have heard
(if not, here's Lesson Two) the pleasure lies

in fingering loose ends toward likely shape,
actually *making something* of these bits
of persons, places, things one finds once one

commences late interrogation
of undervalued, overlooked terrain—
what we in the business like to call *the dig*.

MUSÉE

The old masters? Seldom wrong about *anything*,
never quite able to admit it when they were.

    Notice, please, the execution of the wretched figure

That, I suppose, is the most fraught disadvantage
in being master, especially an old one.

    all but veiled by chiaroscuro and the prominence

Still, when it came to suffering, they had the most
reliable perspective, compelling credentials.

    of the winged tormentors whose features nearly radiate

They came to it, as they came to everything else—
practice, repetition, unwavering habit.

    with pleasure taken in such consummate facility

O, long before they seemed anything like masters
they had come to observe every human torment

    with the ivory hooks, and with the glinting, brazen,

as the fortunate occasion (they were masters)
for their most passionate renderings.

    long-shaft pikes with which they daub the matter near the
    signature.

DEEP BELOW OUR VIOLENCES

Hard to describe, really—little light, no sense
of direction, and a persistent hum
which is almost Tibetan in its rhythms,

its repetition, its *human cum insect* tenor.
Still, there is a path, and though you must
take it with no indication of progress,

you come to believe that things look better
in transit. So you keep going, alert
to any clue as to how things down here

translate into the mess up there, any
possibility that some adjustment
at the hidden base of things might result

in better manners up top where it counts.

Back up in daylight, things are pretty much
how you left them. In a general, average way,
the permanence of the well-fed running

roughshod over the prostrate many
becomes a little hard to watch. The giddy
bloodlettings and pummelings one likes

to euphemize into regional conflict
have acquired a predictability
you'd just as soon be wrong about.

And you come to suspect that events so
common, universally available,
are incorrectly taken as local color.

Up or down, it's all pretty much a puzzle,
and such requests as the *heart of the matter*
or *the root cause* may be best left to those

who like their fictions pretending to be otherwise.

MR. STEVENS OBSERVES THE BEACH

Quite pleasant in its way, its deeply sad,
largely inarticulate way. And what
is that in the air? Some faint and fleeting

eau de decay? Low tide in our shallow bay.
Say, you've got a look about you that suggests
something nearly tropic on your mind.

Listen! A dozen *shes* singing at the shore!
But singing such cacophony you might
mistake the song for some mere calling home

of errant boys, or common hollering
in a game of volleyball, or just loud talk.
A fortunate boundary, don't you think?—

this ample stretch confusing sand and sea.
I like it best just after a good storm
when everything is changed—the wrack

and wreckage newly rearranged, the beach itself
retrenched along an unexpected line.
You can walk for hours before you meet the signs

insisting that the shore is property,
purchased (with a lien) and posted to attempt
some wish for privacy. They don't mean much.

Turn back if you will, I like walking there
best of all, where the illusion of ownership—
soon enough recensed by size 12 loafers—

gives way to more productive misperception.
The lighthouse at the point is miles farther
than it looks. Our sunlight is so keen

it pricks the simplest observation. Down
the windswept margin human figures,
dogs, beached boats, our tufted yellow grasses,

the very dunes, *all* waver in the heat,
all seem—so long as you squint in your approach—
to verge on something large indeed. The sea

has a numbing sort of genius, which it flaunts.
Not far inland, the earth's fixations strike
their grinning pose, frankly idiotic;

but here, where substances continue making
daily messes of all things, where even I
each day discover I am made to make

another set of fresh concessions which,
so long as no one's listening, I like to sing
with some measure of abandon into wind.

INTERVAL WITH ERATO

That's what I like best about you, Erato sighed in bed, *that's why
you've become one of my favorites and why you will always be so.*
I grazed her ear with my tongue, held the salty lobe between my lips.

I feel like singing when you do that, she said with more than a hint
of music already in her voice. So sing, I said, and moved down
to the tenderness at the edge of her jaw. *Hmmm,* she said, *that's nice.*

Is there anything you don't like? I asked, genuinely meaning
to please. *I don't like poets in a hurry,* she said, shifting
so my lips might achieve the more dangerous divot of her throat.

Ohhhh, she said, as I pressed a little harder there. She held my face
in both hands. *And I hate when they get careless, especially
when employing second-person address.* She sat up, and my mouth

fell to the tip of one breast. Yes, she said, you know how it can be—
they're writing "you did this" and "you did that" and I always assume,
at first, that they mean me! She slid one finger into my mouth to tease

the nipple there. *I mean it's disappointing enough to observe
the lyric is addressed to someone else, and then, the poet spends
half the poem spouting information that the you—if she or he*

*were listening—would have known already, ostensibly as well as,
or better than, the speaker.* I stopped to meet her eyes. *I know just
what you mean,* I said. She leaned down to take a turn, working my chest

with her mouth and hands, then sat back in open invitation.
Darling, she said as I returned to the underside of her breast,
have you noticed how many poets talk to themselves, about *themselves?*

I drew one finger down the middle of her back. *Maybe they fear*
no one else will hear or care. I sucked her belly, cupped her sopping
vulva with my hand. *My that's delicious*, she said, *lifting into me.*

Are all poets these days so lonely? She wove her fingers with mine
so we could caress her there together. *Not me*, I said, and ran
my slick hands back up to her breasts. I tongued her thighs. I said, *I'm not*

lonely now. She rubbed my neck, *No, dear, and you shouldn't be.*
        She clenched, *Oh!*
a little early bonus, she said; *I like surprises.* Then, *so*
few poets appreciate surprises, so many prefer to speak

only what they, clearly, already know, or think they know. If I
were a poet . . . well, I wouldn't be one at all if I hadn't
found a way to get a little something for myself—something new

from every outing, no? Me neither, I said, if somewhat indistinctly.
Oh! She said. *Yes!* She said, and tightened so I felt her pulse against
my lips. She lay quietly for a moment, obviously thinking.

Sweetie, she said, *that's what I like best about you—you pay attention,*
and you know how to listen when a girl feels like a little song.
Let's see if we can't find a little something now, especially for you.

THE SUBTLER EXILES

A little etymology can do a lot of harm.
        Turn over any cornerstone you'll find a thousand roots—
Any one of which might prove to be fun pulling up, if sure
        To cause a problem for the Post Office, hardly a treat
For the little tree. Still, exile has its advantages,
        Not the dullest of which is the lip-smacking circumstance

Of owing nothing to anything or anybody—

A banal flavor of freedom, to be sure, but a taste
One might easily enough acquire through repetition.

Being oppressed by snake worshipers is a real drag,
But asserting clear title to disputed wilderness

Won't often result in quiet mornings over tea.
I'd hoped for indication of my getting somewhere,

Which is probably about as likely as nostalgia.
There are other words for most of this. You can look them up.

I found myself saying once how even a simple gesture
Winds up pointing fingers, shirking responsibility;

But even *that* turns out a surprising disappointment
Once you've finished talking and the term is far from over.

So, I've set off again, this time striking out as naked
As I can manage—which is to say, I remain pretty well

Covered up, greatly burdened, oblivious to most of it.

THE ESTUARY

turns out to have been the only way in,
at least the only way in from where
I began—a river pier extending

from borrowed shore beneath a rented house.
Here, the river's current meets the greater
pressures of the bay. As if unwilling

to accept its mingling dissolution,
the river seems to turn against itself,
to boil up into a rage, which makes

you stop and think before you dare to cross
this riptide in your little boat. Me? I kept
the outboard engine roaring in reverse,

not to retreat, exactly, mostly just
to hold my place until progress appeared
more possible. Out beyond the trouble

just before me, the blue expanse lay calm,
and farther out a dozen little boats
sat strangely fixed, their white sails slack, but you

weren't looking for allegory here, so
let's agree that the boats were real boats, that
they lay utterly still upon blue water,

and that for all this unsettling lack
something out there opened to the eye,
something rose and brooded still above the bay,

and in its mute immensity held that span
beyond the bar, where the larger body
met, absorbed our little estuary.

IN THE MINDS OF THREE SISTERS

1. The Believer

Her father has now *gone to be with God*, and so
this emptiness—the body—means very little,
left, as it is, so utterly behind, almost
beneath the dignity of her attention.
She looks from one weeping witness to the other,
and though she is also weeping, she asks them
with her eyes, *Why do you weep? He is not here.*

2. The Unbeliever

This stillness is unbearable, but she will bear it,
will find in time a manner of recalling
the man's dissolution as complete, something
of a relief. He is surely not *beyond* pain,
but the pain is gone—as the life is gone—and his
body rests, cooling, glazed with the last evidence,
last oils, of an impossibly wearied engine.

3. The Other

As he shuts down for good, the room itself goes slack.
What pain he knew has leapt into her throat, and so
she swallows it, and keeps it there to grow into
a kind of dread. She alone will set her lips to his,
and smooth his face, and will retain this bleak tableau
as first communion with the flesh, and with the dire
puzzlement the body held, holds, insinuates.

REGARDING THE BODY

I too was a decade coming to terms
with how abruptly my father had died.
And still I'm lying about it. His death
was surely as incremental, slow-paced
as any, and certainly as any
I'd witnessed. Still, as we met around him
that last morning—none of us unaware
of what the morning would bring—I was struck
by how quickly he left us. And the room
emptied—comes to me now—far too quickly.
If impiety toward the dead were still
deemed sin, it was that morning our common
trespass, to have imagined too readily
his absence, to have all but denied him
as he lay, simply, present before us.

A LIFE WITH ERATO

Dear, she said one day, *I'm weary of all the petty coherences
the public life demands.* By then, I'd grown used to paying
close attention whenever she spoke, and certainly whenever she spoke

in that melancholy tone. *Yes, love,* I said, and saw immediately
how right she was. *Nothing's so futile,* I agreed, *as those scores of
happenstance
hoping to pass themselves off as the big picture. It breaks your heart, really.*

And it must be—I was thinking—far tougher for her, petitioned

as she was by endless requests from haggard men and women who,

for the most part, smoked and drank too much, by and large looked like
       shit,

or, at best, looked as though they'd look like shit very soon. Nearly all

had sour breath, grim dispositions, and a degree of neediness that turned
       out,

finally, to be insatiable. Never, it seemed, did it occur to a single one to
       just shut up.

I heard it all too, of course (I seldom left her side), but it must have
       been far

harder for her, always saying no, knowing they wouldn't hear even that,

but would press on with their doomed compositions until, because they
       were

so many, their exhausted discourse became the fashion, if a dowdy one
       at that,

and threatened to obliterate from view the more, say, spirited work our
       coupling

bore; and, well, it has made for more than a few disappointments over
       the years.

But I've got to tell you, coming home to a woman like that has a way of
       making light

any disillusion in the world at large. She sang. I heard my own voice
       rise to meet her.

   Let's say that the veiled alcove of the private life offered ample
       compensation.

II.
The Recovered Midrashim
of Rabbi Sab

Regarding the sage whom tradition has come to identify as Rabbi Sab, very little is known, though a great deal is suspected. He was apparently a learned man whose devotion to The One Whose Name Is Not Spoken did not preclude his speaking that name frequently, and more often than not accompanied by a tone of accusation. He himself has been accused of apostasy, blasphemy, manic-depression, drunkenness, bad manners. He has been praised for his compassion, revered—if not much liked— for his eager upbraiding of the pious. While most forgive him his denunciations, few forgive him his glee. As to whether the emanation of the dual Torah extends to comprehend even these recovered commentaries, opinions vary.

YHWH'S IMAGE

*And God said, "Let us make man in our image,
after our likeness."*
—Genesis 1:26

And YHWH sat in the dust, bone weary after days of strenuous making, during which He, now and again, would pause to consider the way things were shaping up. Time also would pause upon these strange durations; it would lean back on its haunches, close its marble eyes, appear to doze.

But when YHWH Himself finally sat on the dewy lawn—the first stage of his work all but finished—He took in a great breath laced with all lush odors of creation. It made him almost giddy. As He exhaled, a sigh and sweet mist spread out from him, settling over the earth. In that obscurity, YHWH sat for an appalling interval, so extreme that even Time opened its eyes, and once, despite itself, let its tail twitch. Then YHWH lay back, running His hands over the damp grasses, and in deep contemplation reached into the soil, lifting great handsful of trembling clay to His lips, which parted to avail another breath.

With this clay He began to coat His shins, cover His thighs, His chest. He continued this layering, and, when He had been wholly interred, He parted the clay at His side, and retreated from it, leaving the image of Himself to wander in what remained of that early morning mist.

THE ENTRANCE OF SIN

The man said, "The woman You put at my side—she gave me of the tree, and I ate."
—Genesis 3:12

Yes, there was a tree, and upon it, among the wax leaves, an order of fruit which hung plentifully, glazed with dew of a given morning. And there had been some talk off and on—nothing specific—about forgoing the inclination to eat of it. But sin had very little to do with this or with any outright prohibition.

For sin had made its entrance long before the serpent spoke, long before the woman and the man had set their teeth to the pale, stringy flesh, which was, it turns out, also quite without flavor. Rather, sin had come in the midst of an evening stroll, when the woman had reached to take the man's hand and he withheld it.

In this way, the beginning of our trouble came to the garden almost without notice. And in later days, as the man and the woman wandered idly about their paradise, as they continued to enjoy the sensual pleasures of food and drink and spirited coupling, even as they sat marveling at the approach of evening and the more lush approach of sleep, they found within themselves a developing habit of resistance.

One supposes that, even then, this new taste for turning away might have been overcome, but that is assuming the two had found the result unpleasant. The beginning of loss was this: every time some manner of beauty was offered and declined, the subsequent isolation each conceived was irresistible.

THE TURNING OF LOT'S WIFE

As the sun rose upon the earth and Lot entered Zoar, the Lord rained upon Sodom and Gomorrah sulfurous fire from the Lord out of heaven. He annihilated those cities and the entire Plain, and all the inhabitants of the cities and the vegetation of the ground. Lot's wife looked back, and she thereupon turned into a pillar of salt.
—Genesis 19:23–26

First of all, she had a name, and she had a history. She was *Marah*, and long before the breath of death's angel turned her to bitter dust, she had slipped from her mother's womb with remarkable ease, had moved in due time from infancy to womanhood with a manner of grace that came to be the sole blessing of her aging parents. She was beloved.

And like most daughters who are beloved by both a mother and a father, Marah moved about her city with unflinching compassion, tending to the dispossessed as if they were her own. And they became her own. In a city given to all species of excess, there were a great many in agony—abandoned men, abandoned women, abandoned children. Upon these she poured out her substance and her care.

Her first taste of despair was at the directive of the messengers, who announced without apparent sentiment what was to come, and what was to be done. With surprising banality, they stood and spoke. One coughed dryly into his fist and would not meet her eyes. And one took a sip from the cup she offered before he handed it back and the two disappeared into the night.

Unlike her husband—coward and sycophant—the woman remained faithful unto death. For even as the man fled the horrors of a city's conflagration, outrunning Marah and both girls as they all rushed into the desert, the woman stopped. She looked ahead briefly to the flat expanse, seeing her tall daughters, whose strong legs and churning arms were taking them safely to the hills; she saw, farther ahead, the old man whom she had served and comforted for twenty years. In the impossible interval where she stood, Marah saw that she could not turn her back on even one doomed child of the city, but must turn her back instead upon the saved.

THE SACRIFICE OF ISAAK

They arrived at the place of which God had told him.
Abraham built an altar there; he laid out the wood;
he bound his son Isaak; he laid him on the altar, on top
of the wood. And Abraham picked up the knife to slay
his son.
—Genesis 22:9–10

Who among us could bear the memory of Abraham's knife as it entered the heart of his son? Few enough, presumably. For why else has that incommensurate tableau been misrepeated so thoroughly?

In the stillness of that hour, the Lord pressed his servant inexplicably far and despite the gentled features of a great many fables thereafter—the angel's intercession, the convenient goat, *et cetera*—the knife did find its cramping sheath there in the boy's bared breast, and blood covered both the boy and the father who embraced him even then, and blood colored the rock altar, rouged the mire underfoot.

In pity, then, the Lord briefly withheld time's aberrant fall, retracted the merest portion of its descent, sparked a subsequent visitation of the scene. This time, he stayed the hand, the knife, the rush of blood and of horror, but only in time.

Just outside time's arch embarrassment—in the spinning swoon of the I Am— the boy is bloodied still upon the rock, the man fallen upon him, left with nothing but his extreme, his absolute, his dire obedience.

AT GRIPS WITH JACOB

*Jacob was left alone. And a man wrestled with him until the
break of dawn. When he saw that he had not prevailed against
him, he wrenched Jacob's hip at its socket, so that the socket of
his hip was strained as he wrestled with him. Then he said,
"Let me go, for dawn is breaking." But he answered, "I will not
let you go, unless you bless me."*
—*Genesis 32:25–27*

As the Angel of the Lord stooped to a little sport with the liar, He could not help but smile at how excessively the man struggled, as if he had a chance. And the Angel of the Lord was well pleased by how adroitly Jacob scuttled about in the dust, intent upon finding sufficient leverage, which, of course, he could not do.

During which time the Angel of the Lord continued to assume the man would eventually tire, finally give in to what was obvious, the impossibility of success.

So, when after many days Jacob's tenacity showed no promise of decline, when the Angel of the Lord began to stare a little glassy-eyed at yet another approach by his unlikely rival, when, after having tossed Jacob to his back for the umpteenth time, the man took yet another tack, the Angel of the Lord put an end to the annoyance, hobbling Jacob with a single tap at the hip.

Jacob's sudden agony was a surprise to both. And as the man spun in the dust, tearing up great fistsful of earth, the Angel of the Lord came to suspect a manner of suffering He had not known.

And thereafter, when He had set the hip right, when Jacob lay sleeping, his brow finally smoothed by ease and calming dreams, the Angel of the Lord continued watching, admiring the phenomenon of change, keeping His own counsel as He speculated on the compensating aftermath of anguish, and the man's astonishing ability to be made whole.

IN THE WELL OF JOSEPH'S
BRIEF DESPAIR

When Joseph came up to his brothers, they stripped Joseph
of his tunic, the ornamented tunic that he was wearing, and
took him and cast him into the pit.
—Genesis 37:23–24

From that chill floor whose cloying mud became a numbing garment, the young man saw the world above poised as a pale blue pool—remote and indifferent—which, rather than reflecting any semblance of himself seemed rather to absorb just about everything—all light, all hope, his future. He had tried climbing out, had tried calling for mercy, but each failure had left him more weary, disheartened, more thickly coated with mud.

And in that airless space the taunts and accusations from above also became increasingly confused, so that words became less, less like objects, more like unfortunate weather. Finally, exhausted and utterly without resort, Joseph slid back to the clay, giving in to the pressure of the blue pool held above him, falling silent as its trembling aspect became an abysmal amplitude.

Then he was lifted out, haggled over, and sold for a meager sum, during which time he could neither struggle nor speak. The journey into Egypt was one long study of the sky without conclusion.

And in succeeding years, through their provocative turns of fortune—false accusations, a little stretch in prison, a developing facility with dreams—Joseph came gradually into his own, famously forgave his own, pretty much had the last laugh, save when, always as late in the day as he could manage, he gave in to sleep and to the return of that blue expanse, before which all accretion—accomplishment, embellishment, all likely interpretations—would drop away as he found himself again in the hollow of that well, naked, stunned, his every power spinning as he lay, and looked, and swam.

THE DEATH OF MOSES

The Lord said to Moses in Midian, "Go back to Egypt, for all the
men who sought to kill you are dead." So Moses took his wife
and sons, mounted them on an ass, and went back to the land of
Egypt; and Moses took the rod of God with him. . . . At a night
encampment on the way, the Lord encountered Moses and sought
to kill him.
—Exodus 4:19–20, 24

And in the interval of rest following the Father's tedious conversations with Moses, His own anger at the little man's blithe insubordination became nearly uncontrollable. And the Lord determined to kill the man, thereafter to undertake a more likely deliverance for His people.

Of course, Moses was instantly dead—his insistence upon remaining upright, walking about, chattering on with the innkeeper notwithstanding. For who can live, even briefly, beyond the forbearance of the Lord?

And if he lay dozing after a big meal of charred lamb and crushed mint, and if he lay dreaming of the innkeeper's well-fed wife, who would dare propose that any of these incidentals serve as evidence of life? That he was, despite appearances, breathless is articulated by his ability to sleep at all after such unpleasantness with the Father. He dreamed many dreams—vast chasms, pouring vortices, a single ram tethered to a post of limestone—none of them the dreams of the living.

As we are told, the Lord soon repented of His momentary whim, retracted the death, and, unbeknownst to the man—who, tradition has it, ordered a big breakfast and went his way as if nothing much had happened, pinching the innkeeper's wife on his way out the door—returned Moses to his place among the many other volatile shadows.

SOLOMON'S EROTIC IMAGINATION

Oh, give me the kisses of your mouth,
For your love is more delightful than wine.
Your name is like finest oil—
Therefore do maidens love you.
Draw me after you, let us run!
The king has brought me to his chambers.
Let us delight and rejoice in your love,
Savoring it more than wine—
Like new wine. . . .
—The Song of Songs 1:2–4

To what purpose is the extravagant beauty of the body? To what purpose the lush accompaniment of two bodies drawn into a single contemplation? Solomon, our greatest poet and our king, could not for all his wisdom come to final understanding—for which we are grateful both to Solomon and to the Lord—but came instead to chance elaboration cast in song.

The woman (consider her form and consider what to Solomon would have seemed her implicit willingness) stood before him only once, and, because she was unaccustomed to such attention and because he was stunned into uncharacteristic humility, she stood before him only briefly before she retrieved her robe from where it lay at her feet, slipped back into it, and, promising to return when she was feeling a little braver, exited the tent.

Such modest exposure may not seem much, but for Solomon it proved plenty. And subsequently all of creation—the labor of bees, spice-scented evergreens, the heartrending, frolicking leap of twin deer—spun into serving a manner of expression whose sole outcome was to utter its own insufficiency. For though his song exceeds all songs in addressing the beauty of the woman, it falls silent at its conclusion, as it must, having offered only another manner of poverty *in lieu* of the woman, which it could not touch.

JEPHTHAH'S PIETY

And Jephthah made the following vow to the Lord: "If you deliver the Children of Ammon into my hands, then whatever comes out of the door of my house to meet me on my safe return from the Ammonites shall be the Lord's and shall be offered by me as a burnt offering." Jephthah crossed over to the Children of Ammon and attacked them, and the Lord delivered them into his hands. . . . When Jephthah arrived at his home in Mizpah, there was his daughter coming out to meet him, with timbrel and dance!
—Judges 11:30–32, 34

One shouldn't be surprised at the wealth of explication our captain has provoked—wishful postulations about reprieve, anachronistic constructions of virgin orders, other hedgings—uncanny as it is that our hero and onetime deliverer could be so rash as to strike a no-win deal with the Almighty, unseemly that he would jeopardize his own for a little leverage in war. Even so, like the unfortunate lot of military men who are, in general, given to confusing their own blood lust with the will of God, Jephthah returned from battle with the Children of Ammon not quite satisfied.

Covered with gore and swaggering into the courtyard—which was more than a little cluttered with a career's worth of spoils—the soldier's attention was fixed upon his own open door, eager to see what he could kill next.

As the small figure rushed out—her arms thrown wide, her legs churning—the man was already considering where he might land the blow, or the series of blows, depending upon his pleasure. There was a flashing instant in which he stopped short, stood flat-footed, and puzzled about the tiny throb of recognition which pulsed once or twice behind his eyes. That's when he was pleased that he had made his vow—no more, then, to consider.

Children are always dying, being killed—both in scripture and in fact—though it is our fond habit and protection to euphemize such gestures as *the Children of Ammon* into purely racial information. Just as the girl reached her father, he ran her through with his sword. As a kind of mercy, he took off her head with a neat trick, moving only his wrist, then entered our house to be adored.

JONAH'S IMPRISONMENT

The word of the Lord came to Jonah son of Amittai: Go at once to Nineveh, that great city, and proclaim judgment upon it; for their wickedness has come before Me. Jonah, however, started out to flee to Tarshish from the Lord's service.
—Jonah 1:1–3

What might one then expect when fleeing the Lord's imperative? Well, an obstacle of one or another sort—uneasiness of mind, missed connections, ungenerous companions, perhaps an enormous fish.

That Jonah was without joy at the prospect of Nineveh is well recorded. Less famous is his disinclination for *any* intercourse with unbelievers, whom he, out of habit, identified as the unwashed. From birth, he had been protected from most embarrassments: body odor, poorly cooked food, substandard grammar. And so the Lord, in His compassion, undertook to deliver Jonah from his own sin—not fastidiousness as such, only Jonah's insistence upon it.

His time in the fish's belly was like death. At the very least it *smelled* like death to Jonah. In retrospect, the experience, fully imagined, might still provoke a necessary sense of how the body, unadorned by ointments, oils, or silk is little more than meat, mere meat for fishes. And if, in that confusion of digesting debris, Jonah chose to distinguish himself from other meat, he would have to come up with other criteria, and pretty soon.

Consider any brute swimmer driving with all his energies against the tide; notice how ineffectual (and potentially comic) the effort appears from the chalk white cliffs above. Gross facts aside, the monster was Jonah's deliverance, a more than sufficient transportation to a more likely perspective, from which Jonah was then fully willing to embrace anybody.

EXILE

Here *exactly*—a little elbow room. Here, in this margin of poor housing, harsh climate, and unreliable municipal services—something of a breathing space.

Have you *seen* the faces of the wanderers? Even in the midst of lamentation (especially then), they are radiant, wide-eyed and weeping, open-mouthed, keening at the tops of their lungs, and delirious with joy and purpose.

Even as the familiar supplications for delivery ascend alongside the fragrance of the censers, even as their voices rise to astonishing volume, and a number of garments—for emphasis—are torn beyond repair, even as the ritual of despair attains unbearable pathos, the blessed appear to be taking some pleasure in the whole affair.

They have their etymologies too, after all—Holiness finding at its root a taste for separateness, fragmentation, periodic disruption in the status quo. Of course they are wandering *toward* something, but not in any great hurry.

Soon enough, they will come upon a day when the journey is fully behind them, when their colorful tents will be rolled up for good and left to rot in some outbuilding. Soon enough, the carts and litters will decay, the herds grow fat and unused to travel. Soon enough, the land will pull them in to stay.

And of their exile? Nothing will remain except the memory—fading even so—of a journey and a life with few oppressive properties, a daily jaunt unparceled by either boundaries or taxes—in short, an expansive excursion expressed for a season between the demands of heathen kings and that last, conclusive embrace.

III.
Supplication

THE FOREST OF THE STYLITES

—for Warren Farha

The way had become unbearably slow, progress
imperceptible. Even his hunger had become
less, little more than a poorly remembered myth

of never quite grasped significance. And the field
he now glimpsed far ahead appeared as a failed
forest whose cedars—bleached and branchless—clearly reached

past the edge of his sight. Occasional, erratic
movement at the tops of a few distant trees spun
his bearings some, induced brief vertigo, recalled

to him his hunger, if as a wave of nausea,
which abated, then poured back as he drew near and the trees
transformed to pillars, each topped by an enormous

weathered flightless bird enshrouded in a rag.

TO HIMSELF

When in scripture we first meet God,
apparently He is talking to Himself,
or to that portion in His midst
which He has only lately quit
to avail our occasion.

In prayer, therefore, we become
most like Him, speaking what no one
else, if not He, will attend.
A book I borrowed once taught me
how in the midst of attendant

prayer comes a pause when The Addressed
requires nothing else be said. Yes,
I witnessed once an emptying
like that; though what I saw was not
quite seen, of course. I suspected

nonetheless a silent Other
silently regarding me as if He
still might speak, but speak as to Himself.
That was yesterday, or many
years ago, and if it profit

anyone to imitate the terms
of that exchange, let the prior
gesture be extreme hollowing
of the throat, an inclination
to articulate the trouble

of a word, a world thereafter.

THANKSGIVING FOR A HABIT

Thus unencumbered by method,
the dilettante exegete finds
ample occasion for discourse,

a habit of trusting the mind's
less architectural leanings,
especially troubling Time's

quaint and illusory pattern,
its pretense of ordering. I'm
guessing his happiest moments

occur in appalling, half blind,
otherwise mute speculation
when, glimpsing some textual bind,

he loosens his grip on the matter,
if briefly, recovers in time,
sees as he circumvents terror

a glimpse of enormity. My
best speculation proposes
that this is as close to sublime

matters as any would wish for
so long as one's still doing Time.

THE MORE EARNEST PRAYER OF CHRIST

And being in an agony he prayed more earnestly . . .
—Luke 22:44

His last prayer in the garden began, as most
of his prayers began—*in earnest*, certainly,
but not without distraction, an habitual . . . what?

Distance? Well, yes, a sort of distance, or a mute
remove from the genuine distress he witnessed
in the endlessly grasping hands of multitudes

and, often enough, in his own embarrassing
circle of intimates. Even now, he could see
these where they slept, sprawled upon their robes or wrapped

among the arching olive trees. Still, something new,
unlikely, uncanny was commencing as he spoke.
As the divine in him contracted to an ache,

a throbbing in the throat, his vision blurred, his voice
grew thick and unfamiliar; his prayer—just before
it fell to silence—became uniquely earnest.

And in that moment—perhaps because it was so
new—he saw something, had his first taste of what
he would become, first pure taste of the body, and the blood.

ANOTHER CRUCIFIXION

The last of the three to die was the one
whose harsh words to the rabbi had availed
for the third culprit the astonishing
promise of paradise.

The last of the three could no longer turn
even his head—his body had stiffened.
He did not dare close his eyes again, so
fixed upon the rabbi's face,

which had grown so utterly still, opaque,
that the dying one observed a vivid
mirroring of his own condition there,
or so he imagined,

confused, struggling to see anything clearly.
As that face blurred, he saw beyond to the one
whose shins were that moment cracking across
the flat of a sword.

That man, too, was clearly dead, and if this day
he also swam in bliss, it didn't show.
The dying man would examine the dead
rabbi one more time

if he could, but finally knew the man
was lost to his sight. He felt a tug, far
away (at his feet?) and a blade across
his knees. He heard them crack,

and heard himself cry out (so far away).
Dying, he thought that if he could just glimpse
the rabbi's ruined face, he might suspect
a kingdom even now.

LOVES

Magdalen's Epistle

Of Love's discrete occasions, we
observe sufficient catalogue,
a likely-sounding lexicon

pronounced so as to implicate
a wealth of difference, where reclines
instead a common element,

itself quite like those elements
partaken at the table served
by Jesus on the night he was

betrayed—like those in that the bread
was breakable, the wine was red
and wet, and met the tongue with bright,

intoxicating sweetness, quite
like . . . wine. None of wheat I write arrives
to compromise that sacrament,

the mystery of spirit graved
in what is commonplace and plain—
the broken, brittle crust, the cup.

Quite otherwise, I choose instead
to bear again the news that each,
each was still *itself*, substantial

in the simplest sense. By now, you
will have learned of Magdalen, a name
recalled for having won a touch

of favor from the one we call
the son of man, and what you've heard
is true enough. I met him first

as, mute, he scribbled in the dust
to shame some village hypocrites
toward leaving me unbloodied,

if ill-disposed to taking up
again a prior circumstance.
I met him in the house of one

who was a Pharisee and not
prepared to suffer quietly
my handling of the master's feet.

Much later, in the garden when,
having died and risen, he spoke
as to a maid, and asked me why

I wept. When at *any* meeting
with the Christ, was I not weeping?
For what? I only speculate

—brief inability to speak,
a weak and giddy troubling near
the throat, a wash of gratitude.

And early on, I think, some slight
abiding sense of shame, a sop
I have inferred more recently

to do without. Lush poverty!
I think that *this* is what I'm called
to say, this mild exhortation

that one should still abide *all* love's
embarrassments, and so resist
the new temptation—dangerous,

inexpedient mask—of shame.
And, well, perhaps one other thing:
I have received some little bit

about the glib divisions which
so lately have occurred to you
as right, as necessary, fit—

That the body is something less
than honorable, say, in its
. . . appetites? That the spirit is

something pure, and—if all goes well—
potentially unencumbered
by the body's bawdy tastes.

This disposition, then, has led
to a banal and pious lack
of charity, and worse, has led

more than a few to attempt some
soul-preserving severance—harsh
mortifications, manglings, all

manner of ritual excision
lately undertaken to prevent
the body's claim upon the heart,

or *mind*, or (blasphemy!) *spirit*—
whatever name you fix upon
the supposéd *bodiless*.

I fear that you presume—dissecting
the person unto something less
complex. I think that you forget

you are not Greek. I think that you
forget the very issue which
induced the Christ to take on flesh.

All loves are bodily, require
that the lips part, and press their trace
of secrecy upon the one

beloved—the one, or many, endless
array whose aspects turn to face
the one who calls, the one whose choice

it was one day to lift my own
bruised body from the dust, where—it seems
to me—I must have met my death,

thereafter, this subsequent life
and late disinclination toward
simple reductions in the name

of Jesus, whose image I work
daily to retain. I have kissed
his feet. I have looked long

into the trouble of his face,
and met, in that intersection,
the sacred place—where body

and spirit both abide, both yield,
in mutual obsession. Yes,
if you'll recall your Hebrew *word*

just long enough to glimpse in its
dense figure *power to produce*,
you'll see as well the damage Greek

has wrought upon your tongue, stolen
from your sense of what is holy,
wholly good, fully animal—

the body which he now prepares.

TESSERAE

—for Marcia Vanderlip

In paling sixth-hour light the woman cups
one azure tile fragment as if asking
of its brokenness a sign. The bright

mosaic framed before her far
from finished, she tries positioning
the speck in mind before her hand inclines

to set the fraction as a sum. In time,
this mote of clay-returned-to-element
will serve as iris for the eye

of an impossibly tinted bird
whose gaudy elegance lies entirely
comprised of likewise shattered earthenware,

which, lifted from the heap, articulates
a second purpose, free from more mundane
practicalities, clearly out of nature

sprung into a flight of some duration.

IN LIEU OF LOGOS

Let's suppose some figure more Hebraic
in its promise, more inclined to move

from one provisional encampment
to the next, then discover the effect

wandering tenders even as it draws
the weary hiker on to further

speculation, crossing what has seemed so
like barren country but whose very

barrenness proves a prod for yet another
likely story. The old Jews liked *davar*,

which did something more than just point fingers
to what lies back behind one's fussy, Greek

ontology of diminishing
returns. I have come to like it too, *word*

with a future as dense as its past,
a *Ding Gedicht* whose chubby letters each

afford a pause at which the traveler
rubs his chin and looking up entertains

a series of alternate routes, just now
staying put at the borrowed outpost,

but marveling how each turn of the head
gives way to distance, layers every term

of travel—each terminal—with reprieve,
invites indeterminate, obscure enormity

to gather at the glib horizon's edge.

INTO HELL AND OUT AGAIN

In this Byzantine-inflected icon
of the Resurrection, the murdered Christ
is still in Hell, the chief issue being

that *this* Resurrection is of our aged
parents and all their poor relations. We
find Him as we might expect, radiant

in spotless white, standing straight, but leaning
back against the weight of lifting them. Long
tradition has Him standing upon two

crossed boards—the very gates of Hell—and He,
by standing thus, has *undone Death by Death*,
we say, and saying nearly apprehend.

This all—the lifting of the dead, the death
of Death, His stretching here between two realms—
looks like real work, necessary, not pleasant

but almost matter-of-factly undertaken.
We witness here a little sheepishness
which death has taught both Mom and Dad; they reach

Christ's proffered hands and everything about
their affect speaks centuries of drowning
in that abysmal crypt. Are they quite awake?

Odd—motionless as they must be in our
tableau outside of Time, we almost see
their hurry. And isn't that their shame

which falls away? They have yet to enter bliss,
but they rise up, eager and a little shocked
to find their bodies capable of this.

SHORT TRIP TO THE EDGE

And then I was standing at the edge. It would surprise you
how near to home. And the abyss? Every shade of blue,
all of them readily confused, and, oddly, none of this
as terrifying as I had expected, just endless.

What? You find this business easy? When every breath is thick
with heady vapor from the edge? You might not be so quick
to deny what prefers its more dramatic churning done
out of sight. Enough about you. The enormity spun,

and I spun too, and reached across what must have been its dome.
When I was good and dizzy (since it was so near), I went home.

PHILOKALIA

(2002)

Two loves that are one:
The love of the Beautiful, the love of the Good.

for Marcia and our children

LATE RESULTS

We wanted to confess our sins but there were no takers.
—Milosz

And the few willing to listen demanded that we confess on television.
So we kept our sins to ourselves, and they became less troubling.

The halt and the lame arranged to have their hips replaced.
Lepers coated their sores with a neutral foundation, avoided strong light.

The hungry ate at grand buffets and grew huge, though they remained
   hungry.
Prisoners became indistinguishable from the few who visited them.

Widows remarried and became strangers to their kin.
The orphans finally grew up and learned to fend for themselves.

Even the prophets suspected they were mad, and kept their mouths shut.
Only the poor—who are with us always—only they continued in the hope.

Descents

Dive down into your self,
and there you will find the steps
by which you might ascend.

—Saint Isaak the Syrian

A LOT

A little loam and topsoil
is a lot.
—Heather McHugh

A vacant lot, maybe, but even such lit vacancy
as interstate motels announce can look, well, pretty
damned inviting after a long day's drive, especially
if the day has been oppressed by manic truckers, detours,
endless road construction. And this poorly measured,
semi-rectangle, projected and plotted with the familiar
little flags upon a spread of neglected terra firma
also offers brief apprehension, which—let's face it,
whether pleasing or encumbered by anxiety—dwells
luxuriously in potential. Me? Well, I *like*
a little space between shopping malls, and while this one may
never come to be much of a garden, once we rip
the old tires from the brambles and bag the trash, we might
just glimpse the lot we meant, the lot we hoped to find.

POETICS FOR TWO

In the exclusive schema of her syntax,
my presence was assumed. Despite the many

obvious advantages of that, my own
desires—and you can probably guess them—

went largely unconsidered, and my preference
for promising obscurities—the thin or less thin

veil, the mediating margin introduced
by contrasting shades of rough or fragile

fabric—passed unexamined. The negligée
was frequently neglected altogether,

which made for pure appearances—true enough—
but overlooked the subtler advantages

bound in well-taught cloth. Whatever gain
accessibility enjoyed also served

to deny the more complicated play
of certain tedious labors. Her arms

upraised as she reclined were ample
invitation even so to dismiss the fancy's

solitary musing and partake.

BLESSÉD

By their very designations, we know the meek
are available for all manner of insult,
the poor have no effectual recourse against

---

the blithe designs of the rich, and that enigmatic
crew we recognize as merciful still refuses
to stand up for itself, which makes of them all prime
objects for whatever device the brutes ordain.
In time, they become mute relics for those who mourn.
If any still crave righteousness, they are maligned,
then stuffed with straw and burned, or hacked to bits and
   burned.
If the pure are anywhere present, we wouldn't
know them, which is surely to their advantage. And those
who would make peace are jailed in adjoining cells, simply
dismissed from any arena that matters now.

PROMISE

Someone is to come, is now to come.
—Derrida

"When the Messiah comes," we mumble as we pore
over our knotted and confused translation. Should
we listen we may hear with a blush that begins
in the breast and rises, and seems even to reach
the responsive leaves of the fringe tree overhead.

The responsive leaves of the fringe tree overhead
fly back as if breathed upon, but that is surely due
to the first gust of the gathering storm approaching,
so we are not inclined to make much more of their
quick flight than that, though we may wince under the *new*

compunction—the common failure to make more. How
often and how clearly must we say these words
before we finally hear them, and their weight reveals
what mute hope they must have harbored all along,
and without our notice, which we only now set down?

PUBLIC PRAYER

also much of the liturgy, the great preponderance
of scriptural poetries, most commonplaces
of ecclesiastical proclamation—each of these

can exhibit a generally poor grip on *point of view*
and on *that* element's unforgiving conventions
of address. When the chatty boor who presumes to pray

on our behalf lifts his voice against the ubiquitous
chatter of the mess hall, sanctuary, stadium, *et
cetera*—or worse, lifts his voice against the stillness

a few have hollowed in their hearts *as* prayer, I'm guessing
he might suspect his first mistake, though of a venial
species. Thereafter, as he proceeds to coach The Holy One

in the several ways *He* might pitch in and help, and opts to list
the many ways our congregation might shape up, as the lump
propped up by pulpit, parish committee, and one poorly

translated book keeps talking, any mute monastic in the wings
can see *and* hear that the monologue has drifted fairly wide
of prayer. For starters: when addressing Second-Person Quite

Singular—if Triply so—the less one says the better. The more
he listens up the more he may observe The Other also listening,
Whose attention he would do well not to interrupt.

POSSIBLE ANSWERS TO PRAYER

Your petitions—though they continue to bear
just the one signature—have been duly recorded.
Your anxieties—despite their constant,

relatively narrow scope and inadvertent
entertainment value—nonetheless serve
to bring your person vividly to mind.

Your repentance—all but obscured beneath
a burgeoning, yellow fog of frankly more
conspicuous resentment—is sufficient.

Your intermittent concern for the sick,
the suffering, the needy poor is sometimes
recognizable to me, if not to them.

Your angers, your zeal, your lipsmackingly
righteous indignation toward the many
whose habits and sympathies offend you—

these must burn away before you'll apprehend
how near I am, with what fervor I adore
precisely these, the several who rouse your passions.

THE SPITEFUL JESUS

Not the one whose courtesy
and kiss unsought are nonetheless
bestowed. Instead, the largely
more familiar blasphemy
borne to us in the little boat
that first cracked rock at Plymouth
—petty, plainly man-inflected
demi-god established as a club
with which our paling
generations might be beaten
to a bland consistency.

He is angry. He is just. And while
he may have died for us,
it was not gladly. The way
his prophets talk, you'd think
the whole affair had left him
queerly out of sorts, unspeakably
indignant, more than a little
needy, and quick to dish out
just deserts. I saw him when,
as a boy in church, I first
met souls in hell. I made him
for a corrupt, corrupting fiction when
my own father (mortal that he was)
forgave me everything, unasked.

VISITATION II

So, imagine my chagrin as waking
I startled to find that mute angelic

circle attending my repose. Thus poised,
their aspect was sufficient to imply

authority—well, if authority,
it was a chastened, none-too-happy sort.

As I say, they never spoke, but betrayed
still an ancient indignation. Clearly,

if they shone at all they were radiant
with rage, and if those dried appendages

were wings, my visitors weren't likely
flying anywhere. If they bore a message,

its terms were nothing I cared to apprehend.
I breathed the simplest *Kyrie*, and shrank,

and never looked to see what then became of them
until the pulse of morning brought me back.

ADVENTURES IN NEW TESTAMENT GREEK: *METÁNOIA*

Repentance, to be sure,
but of a species far
less likely to oblige
sheepish repetition.

Repentance, you'll observe,
glibly bears the bent
of thought revisited,
and mind's familiar stamp

—a quaint, half-hearted
doubleness that couples
all compunction with a pledge
of recurrent screw-up.

The heart's *metánoia*,
on the other hand, turns
without regret, turns not
so much *away*, as *toward*,

as if the slow pilgrim
has been surprised to find
that sin is not so bad
as it is a waste of time.

HESYCHÍA

Stillness occurs with the shedding of thoughts.
—Saint John Klimakós

Of course the mind is more often a roar,
within whose din one is hard pressed to hear
so much as a single word clearly. Prayer?

Not likely. Unless you concede the blur
of confused, compelled, competing desire
the mind brings forth in the posture of prayer.

So, I found myself typically torn,

if lately delivered, brow to the floor,

pressing as far as I could into prayer,

pressing beneath or beyond the roar

that had so long served only to wear

away all good intentions, baffling prayer.

Polished hardwood proves its own kind of mirror,

revealing little, but bringing one near

the margin where one hopes to find prayer—

though even one's weeping is mostly obscured

by the very fact and effect of one's tears,

which, for the time being, must serve.

ADVENTURES IN NEW TESTAMENT GREEK: *HAIRÉSIS*

Surely ours would prove a far less tedious faith

all around if even a few among the more

zealous, more conspicuous brethren knew enough

to *make* a good heretic or two. My own glib

trespasses are clear enough, but when we're talking

heresy, I'd like to think I'm siding with the angels.

Hairésis finds its home in choice, in having chosen

one likely story over its more well received

counterpart, whose form—to the heretic—looks far

less compelling. Poor Arius aside, most heretics

have borne their chosen isolation with something like

integrity, and have spoken to *The Good* as well

as they could manage. Most have spoken quite as well
as they could see. And it's not as if any of us
ever had anything like an adequate view.

The benediction I would choose would be the one
invoking *all* the names of God, Who by all
accounts I'm buying spans the gamut,

as well as everything between each slight,
as well as everything beyond. Historically—
which really *has* to be the toughest

circumstance in which to figure Him—, supposition
hasn't always met with sympathy. No,
you don't need me to underscore the poor

reply with which the body has from time
to time addressed its more imaginative
members, but I would admit what shame

we share, allowing pettiness and fear
to acquire the faint patina of a virtue,
butchery, an ecclesiastical excuse.

Does one always make one's choices? From what
universal view of utter clarity
might one proceed? Let me know when you have it.

Even heretics love God, and burn
convinced that He will love them too.
Whatever choice, I think that they have failed

to err sufficiently to witness less
than appalling welcome when—just beyond
the sear of that ecstatic blush—they turn.

SHORE VIEW, WITH FOG

The roaring alongside he takes for granted,
and that every so often the world is bound to shake.
—Elizabeth Bishop

Half of what I see seems patently compliant,
while half denies nearly altogether every
pointed query of the eye. The fog (more strangely,

this quality of leaden light the fog affords)
extends to all debris here at my feet a new,
an unaccustomed vividness—the layered,

pale yellow sand, the pink and rust and coal-black stones,
this tattered sea-wrack ribbon stretching traced
from here to (think of it) clean around our ragged,

bristling continent—*retraced*, every day! And twice!
While half (that would be the first half, mind you) stretches
quite presentably, the balance (which I suppose

the better half) abides beyond the frame. Which is
a shame, given that the eye pores nonetheless
determined, pokes all the more intently under

every half-apparent surface lolling near our
littered shore. Quite a chore—I'm suddenly convinced—
to navigate a gulf whose every gull and piper

thrives on blind, ecstatic flight. Just now a good half
dozen skirt the sheet suspended underneath
their similarly spry and glazed reflections, which

they seem to kiss, repeatedly—an affectionate,
albeit culinary dip to parse the grit
or seafoam, whose every ebb and fall can slow so . . . well,

seductively the pulse. Whatever animating
bits they siphon from the sand must satisfy
intensely—given how they hurry, how they stare.

Conversely, even as I speak, I can't quite shake
vague dissatisfaction as I walk, keep walking,
continue missing half.

THE MODERN POETS

had first to supply as fitting complement
to the plow, the loft, the timid flock an urban
avatar or two, had first to raise the City's
patent mediocrities to roughly Orphic
tenor, even such gross vehicles as Coupes DeVille
and Packards. They had thereafter to endow
with prophetic agency such proximate folk
as sausage vendors, the ubiquitous barkers
of burlesque, the jaundiced hacks. More delicate yet,
if they would succeed our moderns would need resist
as well the wince or smirk regarding all of the above
as lesser vestige of the bygone Bucolic scape.

In this, most would fail, albeit famously,
but a few—and you can probably name them—
would observe among the City's earnest
indigenes and bright machinery an immanence
they would not greet embarrassed, but would esteem.
Upon the span, the tug, among the legion
mazing passages and thriving scenes, these
would entertain a vivid host of angels,
if not quite unawares, would receive as dew the kiss
of sleet, as the murmur of bees the hived drone
of the rain wet El, as incense an idling exhaust.

THREE DESCENTS

1. Aeneas

As the belovéd Palinúrus sank
more deeply beneath wave and memory,
as the remnant of his race descended

painted planks to step on foreign shore
and there spark fire, gather wood and water,
even as the god's red fist fell hard into the sea,

Aeneas pressed through tangled underbrush
to gain the door to hell. First, of course, he found
the temple of another petty god, graved

with images of all that lay ahead—
his fortune and the fate of every soul
he'd implicated in his flight from Troy.

He barely looked, so used he had become
to how little pleasure Time could bring,
so engaged by the prospect of stepping

briefly out of it, if only to return
to Time's demands when he returned to light.
He hurried through the golden vault to find her

whose words would lead him through the awful gates.
And what would he remember years from now
of what he'd find? Little, save the wretched

figure of his own father coupling death,
nearly indistinguishable amid
that mass of shades like dogs tied together,

whining. And the figure of the Sybil
likewise bound, then tossed, a bent toy skipped across
a marble floor, moot refusal widening

her eyes, opening her throat as the god's thin voice
coughed out the infernal terms Aeneas
believed he sought, might welcome, until he heard them.

2. Orpheus

That his eyes positively shone with the image
he had shaped—of sweet reprieve, of his hand upon
the belovéd, lifting her from the narrow crypt

caught floating on barren stillness, unaccustomed
silence—could not be comprehended by those few
whose minds retained a trace of how the present gloom

was nothing of itself but served to amplify
the absence of the luminous occasions worked
above. That his lit gaze upon those shades who lined

the path could hurt them like a flame did not occur
to him, though he observed their trembling as he passed,
had puzzled as they shrank, slipped back into the Dis.

Her tender heel bitten to the bone, the woman
could barely walk the ruined path she followed down,
and as he pressed with greater speed to apprehend

her frail figure hobbled by its crumbling clay, she turned
to understand the source of sudden suffering,
as if a boy had held a surgeon's glass above

a shriveling midge now stricken by the sun's light drawn
and focused to a beam. As their eyes met, her loss
was total and immediate. When he returned

alone to the sunlit world of things, his life
became one long attempt at shaking free his culpability
 in her undoing. And later, as his own flesh

was torn, his body sundered by the famished hands
of famished women, he breathed a last, a single note,
contrite at how his lesser love had hurt her.

3. Jesus

That his several wounds continued to express
a bright result, that still the sanguine flow
coursed tincturing the creases of his cheek

and wended as he walked to bless the bleak,
plutonic path with crimson script declaring
just how grave the way that he had come,

that underfoot the very clay he traveled
sank beneath an unaccustomed weight
occurs as no surprise. That he was glad

is largely otherwise, as would be the news
that every sprawling figure found *en route*
acquired at his approach an aspect far

more limpid than the lot that lay ahead.
As if his passing gained for hell itself
a vivifying agency, each shade

along the way rose startled, blinking, at once
aware that each had been, until this moment,
languishing, until this moment, dead.

Thus, suddenly aware that each among
the withered crowd had by his presence met
a sudden quickening, the multitude

made glad by his descent inclined to join
him on the path recovering each loss,
exulting in each past made newly present.

His etched face luminous and very flesh
made brilliant by the unremitting pulse,
he gains the farthest reaches where the ache

of our most ancient absence lay. He lifts
our mother and our father from beneath
the mindless river, draws them to himself, and turns.

ADVENTURES IN NEW TESTAMENT GREEK: *NOUS*

You could almost think the word synonymous
with mind, given our so far narrow
history, and the excessive esteem

in which we have been led to hold what is,
in this case, our rightly designated
nervous systems. Little wonder then

that some presume the mind itself both part
and parcel of the person, the very seat
of soul and, lately, crucible for a host

of chemical incentives—combinations
of which can pretty much answer for most
of our habits and for our affections.

When even the handy lexicon cannot
quite place the *nous* as anything beyond
one rustic ancestor of reason, you might

be satisfied to trouble the odd term
no further—and so would fail to find
your way to it, most fruitful faculty

untried. Dormant in its roaring cave,
the heart's intellective aptitude grows dim,
unless you find a way to wake it. So,

let's try something, even now. Even as
you tend these lines, attend for a moment
to your breath as you draw it in: regard

the breath's cool descent, a stream from mouth
to throat to the furnace of the heart.
Observe that queer, cool confluence of breath
and blood, and do your thinking there.

HAVING DESCENDED TO THE HEART

Once you have grown used to the incessant
prayer the pulse insists upon, and once
that throbbing din grows less diverting

if undiminished, you'll surely want
to look around—which is when you'll likely
apprehend that you can't see a thing.

Terror sometimes sports an *up* side, this time
serves as tender, hauling you to port.
What's most apparent in the dark is how

the heart's embrace, if manifestly
intermittent, is really quite
reliable, and very nearly bides

as if another sought to join you there.

RECITATION

He did not fall then, blind upon a road,
nor did his lifelong palsy disappear.
He heard no voice, save the familiar,

ceaseless, self-interrogation
of the sore perplexed. The kettle steamed
and whistled. A heavy truck downshifted

near the square. He heard a child calling,
and heard a mourning dove intone its one
dull call. For all of that, his wits remained

quite dim. He breathed and spoke the words he read.
If what had been long dead then came alive,
that resurrection was by all appearances

metaphorical. The miracle arrived
without display. He held a book, and as he read
he found the very thing he'd sought. Just that.

A life with little hurt but one, the lucky gift
of a raveled book, a kettle slow to heat,
and time enough therefore to lift the book

and find in one slight passage the very wish
he dared not ask aloud, until, that is,
he spoke the words he read.

Eventual City

I am of the opinion that He is going to manifest
some wonderful outcome, a matter of immense
and ineffable compassion.

—Saint Isaak the Syrian

EVENTUAL CITY

—like Venice, save
that the canals are scarlet, and decay

impossible, neither are the boats
subject to fatigue, neither are the boatmen

whose broad alae suggest great patience.
Its pure stone rises, immaculate—and new

construction will not impede adjacent
progress. If the bearing of those going on

about their work seems fixed, intent, it is
nonetheless benevolent. The air also

broods, scented, though not so as to cloy.
And rather than paling flesh, the light

extends to it a vivid carnality.
The city is nothing at all like Venice,

what made me think it was? Something—maybe
something atemporal in the pulse, or else

the cool painterly quality the eye
attains during its mute pause at the pier.

Or it could be my confusion underscores
a blurred range of effects the body wakens

under the initial blush of just such gravity
attended by an also unfamiliar readiness.

RUMINANT

When he reads, let him seek
for savor, not science.
—Arnoul of Bohériss

So that was why the monk's thin lips
trembled as he took the holy fruit—
how every word becomes a subtle
flesh whose savor one infers piecemeal
as he . . . ruminates. Near enough.
Swallowing whole is fine for dogs,
but even cattle mark the latent good
of mulling matter over and again
—if never quite *again*, given
that the apparent, local matter
of a word will always promise
in its telling textures to be more
the sort of gum whose sugars will
not quit, nor ever quite hold still.

HOMAGE

As the failing poet entered the hall,
the wealthy rose to honor him, and one
 who had come by accident, also rose.

The poet read an essay he had offered
years before to an even more auspicious
gathering, at a time when both his health

and his pleasure in such affairs were more
robust. He then read several famous poems.
Among the discriminating, some found

the poet's English wanting. Others
whispered no, it was his hobbled speech
that grated, and some observed how frail

he had become, and not just a little
distracted. To himself, the lucky one
who had come more as a matter of chance

corrected them, deciding that the man's
demeanor was like one whose conversation
had turned strangely in, had become something more

like self-examination, though—for once—
without disdain. And that one saw how little
it mattered that the essay was well worn,

and he saw as well how little it mattered
that any of them had come. Attending
the failing poet, he saw finally

how nothing pleased the man so much as the call
of his own voice raised against the hall's dim vault,
unless his pleasure lay in the words themselves,

how first they filled his mouth, then spun
the arc of that great hall for him.

—*for JLB*

ADVENTURES IN NEW TESTAMENT GREEK: *MYSTÉRION*

What our habit has obtained for us appears
a somewhat meager view of mystery.
And Latinate equivalents have fared
no better tendering the palpable
proximity of dense noetic pressure.

More familiar, glib, and gnostic bullshit
aside, the loss the body suffers when
sacrament is pared into a tidy
picture postcard of absent circumstance
starves the matter to a moot result, no?

Mystérion is of a piece, enormous
enough to span the reach of what we see
and what we don't. The problem at the heart
of metaphor is how neatly it breaks down
to *this* and *that*. Imagine one that held

entirely across the play of image

and its likenesses. *Mystérion* is

never elsewhere, ever looms, indivisible

and *here*, and compasses a journey one

assumes as it is tendered on a spoon.

Receiving it, you apprehend how near

the Holy bides. You cannot know how far.

AS WE SEE

*The transfiguration of our Lord—that is, the radiance in which
he was bathed at the pinnacle of Mount Tabor—did not manifest
a change in Him, but a change in those who saw Him.*
—Isaak the Least

Suppose the Holy One Whose Face We Seek

is not so much invisible as we

are ill equipped to apprehend His grave

proximity. Suppose our fixed attention

serves mostly to make evident the gap

dividing what is seen and what is here.

The Book there on the stand proves arduous

to open, entombed as it is in layers

of accretion, layers of gloss applied

to varied purposes, hardly any of them

laudable, so many, guarded ploys

to keep the terms quite still, predictable.

Which is why I'm drawn to—why I love—the way
the rabbis teach. I love the way they read—
opening The Book with reverence for what
they've found before, joy for what lies waiting.
I love the Word's ability to rise again
from chronic homiletic burial.

Say the One is not so hidden as we
are kept by our own conjuncture blinking,
puzzled, leaning in without result. Let's say
the meek, the poor, the merciful all
suspect His hand despite the evidence.
As for those rarest folk, the pure in heart?
Intent on what they touch, they see Him now.

FORMAL BRIEF: THE NAME

Forgive my having recourse just above
to the legalistic idiom. Forgive
my having chosen to pursue a measured
argument—and in such lax verse. Forgive
as well my penchant for ironic tone,
for all my insufficiencies—those few
committed here, the many others, there.

And now that you are thus inclined, extend
the courtesy to those who likewise don't
deserve it. Address the water in the pool
and leaning in forgive yourself. The Name
won't bear repeating—I dare say—without
such kind provision. Even so, The Name
will bear thereafter subtle fruit suffused

beyond our reckoning, which also serves
as sweet inducement to repeat The Name.
Some among the saints have found in time
their prayer avails most palpably in silence,
and some have found a path from mind to heart.
Regarding such, I may have more to say
in future, but let's not hold our breaths.

My own rough habit has led to my preferring
to invoke The Name aloud, to draw its shape
into my mouth, to bring together breath
and tongue, to feel those syllables proceed
as tremor to the port of trembling air,
to hear my own voice colored by The Name,
to taste and see—and *then* to savor silence.

ONCE CALLED, THEREAFTER

. . . spirited from sleep, the astounded soul
Hangs for a moment bodiless and simple . . .
—Richard Wilbur

The suspense is familiar, not likely to last,
but wakens the soul to how fit, how meet remain
the body's modest properties reposed.

The yellow flower—as it happened—became far
more yellow with the sun's approach and, when that fire
first cleared the eastern ridge, poured its light

upon our clearing, upon the thousand golden
stalks, blessed their yellow flower with a yellow light,
and proved a yellow deeper than the eye.

Called back at dawn to their accustomed coupling, both
the ghost and her abundant paramour are pleased
to sustain these kind affections, and proceed

upon the morning as one new, impossible
creature bearing bright burnishments of limb and frame,
bearing also in that flesh its quickening.

ADVENTURES IN NEW TESTAMENT GREEK: *APOCATÁSTASIS*

Among obscurer heresies, this dearest rests
within a special class of gross immoderation,
the heart of which reveals what proves these days to be
a refreshing degree of filial regard.

Specifically, the word is how we apprehend
one giddy, largely Syriac belief that all
and everyone will be redeemed—or, more nearly,
have been redeemed, always, have only to notice.

You may have marked by now how late Semitic habits
are seldom quite so neighborly, but this ancient one
looks so downright cordial I shouldn't be surprised
if it proved genesis for the numbing vision

Abba Isaak Luria glimpsed in his spinning
permutations of The Word: Namely, everything
we know as well as everything we don't in all
creation came to be in that brief, abysmal

vacuum The Holy One first opened in Himself.
So it's not so far a stretch from *that* Divine Excess
to advocate the sacred possibility
that in some final, graceful *metánoia* He

will mend that ancient wound completely, and for all.

MEMENTO

In some circles, skulls still serve as graphic
and conventional choice, especially
when what one hopes to call to mind is *Death's*
indisputable if typically discounted
imminence. Here, in the artist's study
even this diminutive golgotha underhand
can serve as scene for just such fraught locality,

as evidenced by a good dozen such paintings,
famous ones, a spate of lyric, plastic,
and dramatic works, not to mention quite a run
of recurrent nightmare billings. One
particularly agéd practice of the ancient Church
promotes actual discourse with the dead;
we speak of them as if they now might hear us,

and we speak *to* them as if they might care
—and more than that, might speak in our behalf.
The icons of the several saints I love the most
create a vivid gallery—if one in that word's
rarer sense, wherein the blessed reposed within its arc
are the crew in best position to comprehend
the view. *These* surround the shallow altar

where I say my prayers and, if I'm lucky,

where I pray. When I say my prayers, of course,

there is much to remember; when I begin to pray,

far more to forget. In any event, we visit the dead,

and *that* tilt of the head thereafter avails

a curious space, wherein we conceive that we too

rest among them—seated maybe, communing

certainly, though afterwards who can recall

exactly what was shared? I can't imagine

that anything was actually said, even if

in that silent vault they nonetheless seemed to speak.

Each brief visit remains about as enigmatic

as you'd guess—a vivid tableau upon which I

still might gaze, but surely irreducible

to paraphrase. Every altar in our churches bears

a holy fragment—bit of bone, most often—

as testament to the uncommon and genuine

honor in which we hold the body—even

shattered bits of it, even when its habitant has,

for all appearances, gone hence. Each mute relic

serves as token both of death *and* of life's appalling

ubiquity—even there. It helps to bear in mind

the curious and irreparable harm the Crucified

inflicted upon the nether realm when graved

He filled it with Himself, and in so doing, burst

its meager hold and burst its hold on us—all

of which has made the memory of death lately

less grim. *Gehenna* is empty, and tenders

these days an empty threat. Remember that.

SACRED TIME

Not time at all, really, but space
like you don't know, and knowledge there,
in general, finally admits

how meager a consolation
it has been all along. Once
you grow accustomed to the sprawl

and velocity your own mind
articulates (and that queasy
rocking tapers to a hum) you might

have pause to entertain a sense
of presence reaching suddenly,
and now, and deeply, ever so.

POET ASCENDING, WITH SKIS
AND POLES

—for Larry Levis

From the vault of memory,
I prefer one bright and nearly
frozen morning near the ridge
where our broad canyon narrows, lifts,
and fades into the Wasatch
Range's sheerest wall. Just there,
our now-absent-poet, grinning
all the way, was taken up
by chairlift. Slouching, decked
in black leather and black jeans

the belovéd sprawls, a little
out of place; he doesn't mind.
He's eager for the crest, whatever
it will bring.

                Just now, it brings the sun,
a wash of yellow light which first
erupts from white obscurity
nesting at the very edge of sight,
and now pours down, igniting
pines, the slope, igniting even
we who witness its approach. And he
sits golden in that avalanche
of dawn, and now he turns
to face those following. He is
pointing with both poles to what
such willingness can bring, if not
always, if only just
often enough. And this is how
I'll carry him—illumined, rising,
calling us to notice, nodding yes.

COMPASS OF AFFECTION

(2006)

for Marcia, Elizabeth
and Benjamin

BLESSÉD BEING

So few poor among us save   the actual poor, who acquire
in due time a serene dis-   interest regarding whatever
evil tomorrow may bring.   So few among us quite willing
to adopt that poverty   promising to adorn the heart
in efficacious tatter.   And so our being yet looms large
if largely out of reach, yet   retains the tremor troubling
the evening's dim diffusions   enhanced just now by scotch served neat.

Where was I? And where was I   prepared to go? Honest, I'd hoped
by now to have accomplished   a somewhat more reliable
demeanor. I'd hoped by now   to have commenced, at least, to pray.
One day, I hope to do so   free of the incredulous,
glib, incessant columnist   established in his box seat, beaming.
How might one dip beneath that   murmur, descend into a self
unadorned, undistracted,   wholly present to the Blessèd

Being in Whom another   blessèd being comes to be?

NARRATION

This is the abomination. This is the wrath . . .
—W. H. Auden, "For the Time Being"

If, on account of the political situation, the press
has become an increasingly incredible source
of quite palpable frustration, if certain
of our neighbors have been made objects
of suspicion, or have become, themselves,
both irritable and suspicious, if our leaders
address their glib monologues with relative success
to the conspicuously inattentive, if the language
of the tribe has been reduced to far fewer syllables,
and the eyes of the tribe tend to glaze over at the first sign
of a subordinate clause, that is our due. We have long
desired that our confusions abate, regardless.

If certain travelers are now subject to untoward
scrutiny, if their baggage, clothing, and orifices are all
equally fair game, if the poor of other lands fail to figure
in the calculus of the launch, and if our own poor
alternate between suicidal rage and suicidal obesity,
if the water carries a taste of tin, and our daily bread
contagion, these too are just deserts. And yes,
the pattern established by our lately narrower range
of variables has attained the look and the feel of permanence.

We have voted, and have agreed not to suffer
the impractical illusions of an earlier time. Who can blame us?
Who would dare? If we prefer the spoiled child's temper
to actual courage, prefer the pride of the cock to anything
smacking of humility, if we prefer what we call justice
to the demands of mercy, what is that to you?

The kingdom has come. We appear quite taken with it.
For the time being, God's will has acquiesced to our own, at least
in this, the kingdom of anxiety, the only realm we care to know.

BRIEF AGE OF WISDOM

Its beginning was the day embarrassment
sat you down, hard, banging your knees against
the tiny desk, the day all your answers—
though good as any—were not good enough.

Stunned as Mr. Reichmann aimed his finger
at your heart, you finally caught his curt demands
for compliance, blithe conviction concerning certain
established tables—multiplication?

periodic? Fictions unambiguous,
and fixed, constructions of self-evident
importance—but far beyond you, apart
from you, your playmates, the girl you addressed

from a distance during recess. Yes, somewhat
clearer now. First taste of a compelling
humility that might have led somewhere,
this suspicion, this beginning and last chance.

TROUBLE

Easy enough to ignore in the glare
of daylight's demanding distractions, chores
which comprise the care, feeding, general
hosing down of our children, the stooping,
clearing of decks, the specific, endless
pinching from the carpet the scraps, debris,
baffling residue of life with children.

But when they finally descend (and so
abruptly) into their disturbingly deep
drowse, when the house is about as tidy
as it will ever be so long as they
live in it, when suddenly you are caught
standing in the middle of the dim room,
surprised to find nothing in your hands . . .

BAD THEOLOGY: A QUIZ

And lo, the angel of the Lord came upon them,
and the glory of the Lord shone round about them:
and they were sore afraid.

Whenever we aver "the God is nigh,"
do we imply that He is ever otherwise?

When, in scripture, God's "anger" is said
to be aroused, just how do you take that?

If—whether now or in the fullness—we
stipulate that God is all in all, just where

or how would you position Hell? Which
is better—to break the law and soothe

the wounded neighbor, or to keep the law
and cause the neighbor pain? Do you mean it?

If another sins, what is that to you?
When the sinful suffer publicly, do you

find secret comfort in their grief, or will
you also weep? They are surely grieving;

are you weeping now? Assuming *sin* is *sin*,
whose do you condemn? Who is judge? Who

will feed the lambs? The sheep? Who, the goats?
Who will sell and give? Who will be denied?

Whose image haunts the mirror? And why
are you still here? What exactly do you hope

to become? When will you begin?

SETTING OUT

Pilgrim: What is it that you do here?
Monk: We fall, and we get up again.

In time, even the slowest pilgrim might
articulate a turn. Given time enough,

the slowest pilgrim—even he—might
register some small measure of belated

progress. The road was, more or less, less
compelling than the hut, but as the benefit

of time allowed the hut's distractions to attain
a vaguely musty scent, and all the novel

knickknacks to acquire a fine veneer of bone-
white dust, the road became then somewhat more

attractive, and as the weather made a timely
if quite brief concession, the pilgrim took this all

to be an open invitation to set out.

AGAINST JUSTICE

*Do not say that God is just; His justice
is not in evidence in His dealings with you.*
—Saint Isaak of Syria

As the day is storm-begotten, so its luminous effects
attain a frankly horrifying face, and every burst arrives
accompanied by rain so sharp it bites the pilgrim's back,
and drives him helplessly away from what has passed for home.
What has passed for home recedes along a washed-out bed
whose bank has over time acquired a grim array—particulate
debris and silt, the scattered wrack that might yet bear a body's

pause, a body's mute reflection. But chalk all that to weather,
and to the sure erosion of the road, and to the chore
of passing on, of suffering the trek from here to there. It's all
a little wild, and all a little slow, and everything
takes on the feel of slightly arbitrary choice, and not just
a little pointless. I'd felt that much of this had more to do
with circumstance, and to the pilgrim's sometimes solipsistic bent,

than to the necessary wage of anxious undertaking.
Yes, I know the poem is difficult, but far more likely to be read
than any script the habits score. The chore, as I've suggested,
lies in tracing any solid thread between the outcome
and its cause, any lead, or leading proposition posed
so as to offer what might pass for revelation. The God
is hardly just, and we are grateful for His oversight.

TWO ICONS

I. Nativity

As you lean in, you'll surely apprehend
the tiny God is wrapped
in something more than swaddle. The God

is tightly bound within
His blesséd mother's gaze—her face declares
that *she* is rapt by what

she holds, beholds, reclines beholden to.
She cups His perfect head
and kisses Him, that even here the radiant

compass of affection
is announced, that even here our several
histories converge and slip,

just briefly, out of time. Which is much of what
an icon works as well,
and this one offers up a broad array

of separate narratives

whose temporal relations quite miss the point,

or meet there. Regardless,

one blithe shepherd offers music to the flock,

and—just behind him—there

he is again, and sore afraid, attended

by a trembling companion

and addressed by Gabriel. Across the ridge,

three wise men spur three horses

towards a star, and bowing at the icon's

nearest edge, these same three

yet adore the seated One whose mother serves

as throne. Meantime, stumped,

the kindly Abba Joseph ruminates,

receiving consolation

from an attentive dog whose master may

yet prove to be a holy

messenger disguised as fool. Overhead,

the famous star is all

but out of sight by now; yet, even so,

it aims a single ray

directing our slow pilgrims to the core

where all the journeys meet,

appalling crux and hallowed cave and womb,

where crouched among these other

lowing cattle at their trough, our travelers

receive that creatured air, and pray.

II. Dormition

Most blessed among all women and among
the mass of humankind,
in this fraught image our mother is asleep.

She lies arms crossed and, notably, across
the spacious foreground
upon an altared bed, her head upraised

upon a scarlet robe,
and we surround her strange repose perplexed
by grief that couples homage

nonetheless. Not we, exactly, but our holy
antecedents, whose bright
nimbi gleam undimmed despite their weeping.

Here again the icon serves
to limn the artifice of time, drawing
to this one still point a broad

synaxis of the blessed, including some
whose souls unbodied have
preceded her to Paradise. Most are bent

in sorrow; several raise a hand to meet
fresh tears. They mourn the dire
severing of blesséd soul from blesséd body.

Leaning in, Saint Peter
lifts the censer with a prayer. Saint Andrew
nearly falls upon the bier.

Saint James Alpheus looks away, or looks

for solace to Saint Luke,

whose eyes—like those of Saints Heirthéus

and adjacent brother James—

direct us to the cupola behind our grief,

from which the risen Christ

attends the mother's solemn funeral

even as he bears her

gleaming spirit in his arms, where she,

so meek the weeping pilgrim might have missed her,

rests swaddled in her shroud,

waiting to be borne to Him, and bodily.

CHRISTMAS GREEN

Just now the earth recalls His stunning visitation. Now
the earth and scattered habitants attend to what is possible: that He
of a morning entered this, our meagered circumstance, and so
relit the fuse igniting life in them, igniting life in all the dim
surround. And look, the earth adopts a kindly áffect. Look,
we almost see our long estrangement from it overcome.
The air is scented with the prayer of pines, the earth is softened
for our brief embrace, the fuse continues bearing to all elements
a curative despite the grave, and here within our winter this,
the rising pulse, bears still the promise of our quickening.

A PRIOR DESPAIR

—after Kavafy

When I saw that I had lost her   completely, I sought the dulcet
taste of her on the lips of each   subsequent woman, her fragrant
flesh in the fold of every lover's   nape thereafter, and her heat
welling with my own and drawing   out an urgency in each
ambiguous woman met   in that tortured interim.

When I saw that I had lost her   I was lost, and held
my eyes shut tight that I might so   delude my wits as to trust
that it was she receiving me,   that it was she returning
with delight the urgent drive   against the unbearable
distance—two bodies, struggling   toward agreeable repose.

Then, tasting once a sudden kiss   so suddenly presented,
I saw another prospect rise   to view, and knew reprieve
from the familiar ring of hell,   from which I rose and marveled
at the offer of another life   whose heat and heady fragrance
rose, delirious to burn   deliciously, and not consume.

SHORT LYRICS

—after Seferis

Turning Point

When the stillness (sent
by what hand?) finally
settled here in my breast
as a mute, black dove, or

210

as a coal, glowing
without color or light,
and the road opened
before me, and the crust

of bread in my mouth
softened with that wine, you,
stillness I have desired,
woke me, deeply.

Slowly

Before the sun, you spoke
as darkness hovering,
pressed our embrace
into something more

than embrace, and even
now, I remember
the sensation like a taste,
a vague ache.

Where is it now, that
savor and moment
when our common breath
drew these thirsts together?

Her Sorrow

Upon the flat stone, longsuffering,
she sits awaiting evening,
the black coals of her eyes
radiating grief (do you feel it?)

her lips a scarlet line,
naked and (do you see?) trembling
as her soul dizzies, her entire
body sobs one plea,

her mind the well, inexhaustible,
from which her tears
draw hot supply, though she
had so nearly turned again,

but her sorrow, thus embraced,
becomes what fills
the night's expanse
with (see them?) so many eyes.

Carriage

Down the rush of road and open
to each intersection's parting
of the way—the wind caressing the hair,
the miles filling our bellies—

we two fled, emptying, frantic
for affection—the mind's áffect, the blood's,
both failing, leaving us exposed,
and each a sparking nerve.

. . . drawn together, once, in bed, the pillow
raised and airy, the scent
of our confusion, and all separateness
slipping away into its bleak sea . . .

Dim, forgetful, we slogged
along our separate roads,
parting, unaware, dis-
embodied, thick with isolation.

Late Denial

In the secret cove,
sands white as dove-down,
we parched, and the water
was useless—half salt, half sweet.

On evening's gilded, ruddy sand,
we etched her name,
but the sea-wind rose
and the script was taken elsewhere.

With what wild craving, hot breath,
what lush ecstasies we pursued
our union there—apparent error.
Chagrined we turned away.

COMPANIONS IN HADES

. . . but he deprived them of the day of their return.
—Odyssey

We ignored our meet provisions—
fools that we are, and faithless—
and disembarked to partake
of what was available and slow,

consuming in haste
and thoughtlessly the elements
we might have honored, and by
so doing, honorably won.

Surrounded by life we swallowed
death. We gorged on it,
and settled in these dim regions,
regardless, grinning, full.

LATE APOCALYPSE

And I turned to see the voice that spake with me.
And being turned, I saw . . .

Blessed is anyone who reads much of anything, blessed
and most unusual. And blessed be the one who gleans
from any text or texture of the latter day a word
of prophecy. As for they who keep those things
they read, they are abundantly blessed and of very
little consequence. The world—impossible conceit—
dwindles in its substance even as its matter flourishes,
and those who might direct it otherwise would be the last

to jimmy up the works that keep them fed and keep

their pampered offspring buffed and quite oblivious

to the evil they perform, the evil they rely upon.

And we, the *remnant ineffectual*, fare hardly better, being

chagrined and silenced by effusive ignorance our own

kind yammers, and choking back our rage at the blithe

demeanor of the opposition. I turned and saw before me

seven bright convenience stores, each laden with a hoard

of sugars and of oils, fuels devised by economics to obtain

the most satisfaction with the least actual good. I turned

and saw before me seven military vehicles in black

and red and yellow, each driven by an unattractive man

or a highly polished woman. I turned and saw before me

seven Wal Marts in a row, and, lo, flowing in and out their doors

a multitude—likened unto apes, corpulent, unhealthy apes,

circus animals towing their young, slapping them every seven

steps or so, schooling them in how they too might one day

bequeath such systematic self-destruction as a sole inheritance.

I turned and beheld seven rows of plasma screens, each bearing

seven vivid scenes, each flickering, each pulsing with a light

revealing distant terrors, conflagrations, sufferings—and all

thereby brought so close, and all thereby kept far away.

I did not turn, but heard from behind a voice like a golden horn

assuring that the image and the sound would prove of highest quality.

THE LEPER'S RETURN

—a gift of Saint Francis

He had grown used to the fear he brought
to every soul he passed along the road,
though the chagrin he bore inside became

a bitterness worse than the fetid taste
that never left his mouth. He could not bear
to stay near town for long, nor could he yet

walk far enough away. His days were marked
in varied degrees of suffering, varied
degrees of shame. So when the brilliant youth

stood trembling, waiting in the road ahead,
he felt the weight of his long burden briefly
lift, and when the youth rushed to embrace him,

the leper startled to discern his body
gently held, and held in firm, benevolent
esteem, and when he felt the kiss across

his ruined cheek, he found forgotten light
returning to his eyes, and looked to meet
the brother light approaching from the young man's

beaming face. Each man blessed the other
with this light that then became the way,
thereafter, each would travel every road.

NOTE

how on occasion
the treble clef turns
triply cleft, troubling

the air imparted
of an evening
to the page. The score

thus parsed amplifies
what polyphony
the ear has lately

apprehended, just
beneath the hearing,
tutoring the hand.

So, every note might
yield its own surround,
intone its own implied

accompaniment,
each note of which might
also launch a layered

orchestration, which
subsequently grants
another measure

yet, and endlessly.

—for JAC Redford

217

IN REFERENCE TO HIS ANNUNCIATION

—apology for Primo Levi

I am sorry for your ancient
       pain, and for your more
contemporary suffering
       which extends impossibly
beyond my knowing.
       I stand chagrined by the brittle
edge our common history
       has honed upon your vision,
and by the way this long
       and righteous rage has served to chill
certain human sympathies.
       Our wretched circumstance
has left you—not for nothing—
       with so little pleasure
in the pulse of those around you.
       And if these words
bear now a trace of censure,
       forgive me all the more.
I have no agency to apprehend
       the world's appearance
before your burning eyes.
       I am most sorry for the tin
taste of righteousness,
       self-assigned, which can taint
the purest waters, and
       —it would appear—nearly any cup.

EURIPIDES THE ATHENIAN

—after Seferis

He found old age awaiting him   on a spare and limpid plain
    between Troy's embers and the mines'   tall white plume near Sicily.

He craved damp caves along the shore,   and would fix for hours upon
    complex oils of the sea, that chaos   of light where sea met sky.

Years before, when he first discerned   the fine veins of *ánthropos*
    proved nets strung by impassive gods   to gather him, and to bind,
    he'd cut his heart to shreds trying   to escape that ancient craft.

His end? Soured to the core, and blind,   alone. When the Fates were done
    with him, even they turned away,   that he be torn apart by dogs.

THE RIGHTEOUS MAN OF GOMORRAH

And when he woke he lay confounded on the plain,
    his body blistered, burnt, encrusted in a husk
        of salt, which crazed and fell from him as he sat up.

Around him all the city lay erased, and he
    sat blinking in a sparkling plain of bitter dust.
        And then the rains began. Their touch upon his flesh

was both exquisite and a searing pain, and woke
    the man more fully to the spanning wreck. He called
        the names of wife and child. Neither merited reply.

And when a sea arrived to glut that blank expanse,
    he named it *Met*—because it bore in tepid depths
        the death of all he cherished—then drank his fill of it.

ICONS

As windows go, these ancient
gilded figures both receive
our rapt attention and announce

a subtle reciprocity.
We look to them to apprehend
a glimpse of life enduring

out of time; and likewise find
our own experience attended
by a tranquil gaze that turns

increasingly affectionate,
indulgent, kind. The stuff of them
—the paint, the wood, the lucent

golden nimbi—also speaks
in favor of how good
all *stuff* remains despite our long

held habits of abuse, disinterest,
glib dichotomies dividing
meager views of *body* and its

anima. On his knees, the pilgrim
leans into another mode
of being, leans into the stillness

at the urgent source of life.
On his knees, the pilgrim meets
the painted gaze, and finds his own

sight answering a question
now just coming into view.

NO HARBOR

What if he *did* attain the long-
desired harbor? What if at last
he came to rest? The stillness

of that projected circumstance
revealed just why his most beloved
theologies would not exactly

satisfy, why allegory
proved so sure to sink the heart
in shallow waters. The ship

with its unfathomed hold
of dim provisions asked for more
than this. No final harbor, nor

the glib assurance of the pier,
but something inarticulate
and . . . well . . . inexhaustible.

He'd meant to keep things moving,
even so, but found his options
worn a little thin, and tinny

both in tenor and in tone. Terror
sports a patent inconvenience,
true enough, but stands regardless

in an absolutely brighter light
than calm, smug and over-fed.
The dead would surely tell him,

if he'd ask them, that the play
of giddy theater extends
beyond the grave, continues

unabated, unconstrained,
extends beyond the fairest
guess, and well beyond his dream.

IN HOPE OF RECOLLECTION

It may not be so much
that *mind* appears so poor
a late translation of
the troubled *nous*. Could be
that what can pass these days
for *mind* among us has
grown so thin, un-bodied.
If thought alone results
from that grey organ's urge
and agency, I'd say
your organism's
fairly screwed, or unfairly,
and you are frankly stuck
with faulty gear. Cheer up,
we've all been there; and look!
it may play out to be
just where we now begin.
I have a hunch our hope
rests yet in moving on,
in acting pilgrim to

another way that might
just lead to something like
reunion with the strewn
self's past constituents.
I had a vision once
of light, or was it heat,
or one brief pulsing stutter
—as a hummingbird
visiting my chest quite near
the heart. You will believe this
or you won't. I thought at first
I was in trouble. Then
I knew I was, but found
that forlorn circumstance
suddenly amenable.
I stopped and stood, leaning in
for what seems now no time
at all, palm to chest, confused
at what it might have been.
The icons on the wall
held still. The vigil light
also held its steady flame.
If I was changed, I couldn't
say exactly how. I'll chance
though, in the interim,
the pulse itself has kept me,
similarly, on certain,
fortunate occasions,
thus mindful, still.

HIDDEN CITY

. . . that you might approach the Jerusalem of the heart . . .
—Isaak the Least

And now I think Jerusalem abides untouched,
the temple yet intact, its every cornerstone
in place, its vault replete with vivid scent, its ark

alight with vigil lamps whose oil is never spent.
In psalm the pilgrim asks forgiveness, pleads that God
return the Spirit to the heart, and look, the Ghost

had never left, had never for an instant drawn
away, had only watched His presence made obscure
by soul's own intermittent darkening. Just so,

the three companions of the Lord had blindly walked
the lesser part of three dim years before their eyes
beheld the Light that bathed the Son eternally.

Just so, the Light of Tabor spools extending past
the vision of the multitude, if nonetheless
apparent to the meek, the poor, the pure in heart.

Just so, the Holy City bides within the heart,
awaits the day the pilgrim will arrive, will quit
the road, turn in to greet his City's boundless sweep, and see.

LATE SOUNDING

So much of what the sea has suffered
is laid upon the shore, so much of what
we lose to it returns, dropped into our laps

unrecognizable, ruined or worked to artifact.
The little skiff I rowed until my arms were sore
is by now parsed to glib constituents, broadcast

in a ring around the calm abyss of our modest
Hood Canal. The shore has long proved adequate
to hold the millings of the sea, at least those bits

it doesn't swallow whole. What's left are these
smooth tokens and, with them, a lucent store
of fragments raised from memory's cool vault—

bright mornings pulling at the oars to check the pots,
the race to meet my mother at the pier, and one
long day adrift and waiting for my father to return

from salmon fishing with Hap and Uncle Ray.
To touch those moments now is hard, and made
more difficult with every passing bier, as we

attend our own slow dissolution, worn, and leaning in.

AUTOPSY

—after Elytis

And look, just beneath the skin, a most challenging stratum
of cedar bark ribbons, overlapping
as if one were thatching a longhouse or hut.

His heart, laid open, revealed a dense island of evergreens and mist.
His entrails had become the stuff of heavy cloud or wood-
smoke maybe, and there, farther down, an alder fire raging.

At the section of one lung, a raven's cry escaped, then
from the other, the gull's complaint. Those who heard this,
began to hasten their grim work. His eyes

that never could quite focus on anything near, continued
with their search, as a shaft of light descending
through storm. Lifting one retina, they found within

a cluttered reliquary—beneath its twin, a vacant tomb.
The ears proved unfathomable, each a salty bay, still
visited by the tide and scuttling, hidden life. When finally they reached

the gray matter packed within, they found a parched desert whose sands
yet gripped the bones of a fallen monk. He appeared
to have failed—and just here—in the very midst of prayer.

REPLIES TO THE IMMEDIATE

No, he mumbled from the podium, the poems
are not my songs. A breeze
troubled the papers in his hands, and a shift
in the air also sent

---

a wave across those seated, tossing their hair,

their broad lapels, their scarves.

The programs in their hands also whispered. Nor,

the man continued, nor

are they my prayers. At that word, the air grew still,

and across his face passed both

a tremor and a calm. Song, he said, attains

to a condition the poem

dare not attend. And prayer? Who would frame a poem

when he had better find

his knees, in silence, having put his art away?

EVENING PRAYER

And what *would* you pray in the troubled midst

of this our circular confusion save

that the cup be taken away? That the chill

and welling of the blood might suffer by His

hushed mercy to abate, to calm the legion

dumb anxieties as each now clamors

to be known and named? The road has taken

on, of late, the mute appearance of a grief

whose leaden gravity both insists on speed

and slows the pilgrim's progress to a crawl.

At least he's found his knees. I bear a dim

suspicion that this circumstance will hold

unyielding hegemony until the day.

What *would* you pray at the approach of this

late evening? What ask? And of whom?

SECRET POEM

—after Seferis

Yes. I have seen the end, and yes
I was disturbed by what I saw.
That I yet glimpse occasional
and frankly stirring satisfactions
in the way the paper draws the ink
may prove one mode of consolation.

That I continue to appreciate
a morning walk, an evening's
intercourse should also speak
encouragement, no? The end
appalls. Quite so. Though I wouldn't say
the end appalls more fully

than the interim. The present
situation—electoral
absurdity, real TV, unprovoked
slaughter thoroughly explained—such
assaults attain a state insisting
that the end arrive, and quickly.

The past is ever with us, but most
have pared it to a less demanding
heft, utilitarian. For me, the past
has become lately my own
articulation of that scene
I saw, just now, as very like the end.

SEPTEMBER 11

And the pillar of fire, and the pillar of cloud
Did not depart from before the people.
—Exodus 13:22

According to the promise, we had known
we would be led, and that the ancient God
would deign to make His hidden presence shown
by column of fire, and pillar of cloud.

We had come to suspect what fierce demand
our translation to another land might bode,
but had not guessed He would allow our own
brief flesh to bear the flame, become the cloud.

IDIOT PSALMS

(2014)

HIGH PLANE

As a field of snow, as a field of Arctic ice, the clouds
below attain, appear to frame, an endless span of white,
of textured white addressed by shades of blue, by varied shades
of what is very nearly blue infused clean into the very clouds,
into their white. What firmament is this? What waters? What
manner of divide? Close your mouth, and open up the stingy
air-vent overhead. Take your whiskey neat, or with a single
chip of ice. Have some nuts. The sun is slipping to the west,
and we rush east, toward night. Our flight is sure to meet the sun
some distance hence, and we are sure to take that puzzlement and all
adjacent puzzlements in stride. Meantime, do have another sip,
and savor this odd margin merging both our waters, merging
what might prove this night to be the mind's late opening occasion.

I.
Unawares

PARABLE

To what might this slow puzzle be
    compared? The rabbi is perplexed.

That said, please bear in mind the rabbi
    has a taste for fraught perplexities.

Comparisons have long obtained
    for those enamored of the word

a measure of requital, have
    tendered—just here, for instance—a

momentary take, a likely
    likening, not to be unduly

honored as anything, well,
    conclusive, but categorically

toward. Still, I love these textures
    on the tongue, and love the way

their taste and feel so often serve
  to spin the body and the mind

into one vertiginous
assemblage. And so, one asks, to what

slight figure might The Vast and
  Inexplicable compare? A mist

that penetrates the bone? The looming
  sea? The all but endless and

unyielding green expanse above?
  Or, say, the laden word whose compass

and whose burdens turn a multitude
  of keen articulations, full

none of which quite seems to satisfy.

THRENODY

The dream is recurrent, and yes
the dream can leave me weeping,
waking with a start, confused,
and pressing my wet face hard
into the pillow. That is to say
the dream is very bitter.

The scenes are various, the gist
unchanging: my father returns,
and we all are at once elated
that his death was apparently
an error, that he had simply
been away, a visit to the shore.

Then, increasingly, I grow
uneasy about how deeply
he has changed. He is both frail
and distracted (or it could be
that he withholds some matter
habiting his mind), and none of us

dares speak, neither of his death nor
of his sudden, startling return.
We share other confusions as well:
He has arrived in the camper truck
he drove when I was a boy, but my wife
and children are also here to greet him,

even my son, whom he has never met.
Often, in the dream, I am the one
who first suspects he cannot stay.
I am the one who sees but cannot say
his visit will be brief. And just
as I suspected, as I feared, I wake.

IRREDUCIBLE IS WHAT I'M AFTER,

which is why I cannot mind so much observing
how words are more precise or less precise, but they
are not exact. Not ever. No. And yes, each proves
solicitous and pleasant on the tongue, and more
than a little tolerant of one's most earnest
yammering; still, the promise of each word abides
within its endless, inarticulate expanse,

thank God. The dancing figures of the utterance
      forever spin their circles; they forever turn
upon the sawdust littered floor. And even as
      I speak I see my good intentions leaping clean
beyond my reach, and each for its duration lifts
      the stillness into trouble. For its bright moment,
each obtains for each a little taste of what lit
      distance one might entertain, thus irreducible.

A WORD

She said *God. He seems to be there*
when I call on Him but calling
has been difficult too. Painful.

And as she quieted to find
another word, I was delivered
once more to my own long grappling

with that very angel here—still
here—at the base of the ancient
ladder of ascent, in foul dust

languishing yet at the very
bottom rung, letting go my grip
long before the blessing.

—for A.B.

IDIOT PSALM 1

—a psalm of Isaak, accompanied by Jew's harp

O God Belovéd if obliquely so,

    dimly apprehended in the midst

    of this, the fraught obscuring fog

    of my insufficiently capacious ken,

    Ostensible Lover of our kind—while

    apparently aloof—allow

    that I might glimpse once more

    Your shadow in the land, avail

    for me, a second time, the sense

    of dire Presence in the pulsing

    hollow near the heart.

Once more, O Lord, from Your Enormity incline

    your Face to shine upon Your servant, shy

    of immolation, if You will.

FIRST STORM AND THEREAFTER

    What I notice first within

        this rough scene fixed

    in memory is the rare

        quality of its lightning, as if

    those bolts were clipped

        from a comic book, pasted

    on low cloud, or fashioned

        with cardboard, daubed

    with gilt, then hung overhead

        on wire and fine hooks.

What I hear most clearly
             within that thunder now
is its grief—a moan, one long
             lament echoing, an ache.
And the rain? Raucous enough,
             pounding, but oddly
musical, and, well,
             eager to entertain, solicitous.

No storm since has been framed
             with such matter-of-fact
artifice, nor to such comic
             effect. No, the thousand-plus
storms since then have turned
             increasingly artless,
arbitrary, bearing—every
             one of them—a numbing burst.

ANOTHER ROAD HOME
—after Stevens

It was when he said expansively *There is*
no such thing as the truth that his thick thumbs
thickened and his lips, purple as grapes,
further purpled. When I thereafter also spun
such spinning facilities as these, my own
vines ripened with what I hoped might prove

more promising fruit. *Γιός μου*, set the large
man's handsome books aside and sit with me
on the airy balcony beside our kind
and loving Father Iákovos. Truth may
prove to be no such a thing as matter
for our mulling; still, this evening spread out

before our mountain, above our mountain tea
suggests in its late, cypress scented air
a pressing density, a wine-like, whelming
cup, *κσινόμαυρο*—deep and dark, substantial.
And the road? Meandering, manifestly
inconclusive, and for that reason not
so likely to ferment blithe disregard.

Γιός μου — yeeóz moo — my son
κσινόμαυρο — kseenómavro — "sour black" a grape indigenous to Greece

AND WHY THEOLOGY?

—because the first must be first
—Milosz

And the first, if you don't mind my saying, is both an uttered
notion of the truth and a provisional, even giddy apprehension
of its reach. The day—quite fortunately, a winter's day—is censed
with wood smoke, and the wood smoke is remarkably, is richly
spiced with evergreen; you can almost taste the resin.

Or, I can. Who knows what you'll manage? The day itself
is shrouded, wrapped, or tucked, say, within a veil of wood smoke
and low cloud, and decidedly gray, but lined as well with intermittent,
slanted rays of startlingly brilliant, impossibly white light—just here,
and over there, and they move a bit, shifting round as high weather

shoves the clouds about. Theology is a distinctly rare, a puzzling
study, given that its practitioners are happiest when the terms
of their discovery fall well short of their projected point; this
is where they likely glimpse their proof. Rare as well
is the theologian's primary stipulation that all that is explicable

is somewhat less than interesting. In any case, the day
keeps loping right along, and blurs into the night, which itself
will fairly likely press into another clouded day, *et cetera*.
The future isn't written, isn't fixed, and the proof of that is how
sure we are—if modestly—that every moment matters.

Take this one, now. We stand before another day extending like
a scarf of cloud, or wood smoke, or incense reaching past what's visible.
And sure, you could as easily rush ahead, abandoning what lies in reach
in favor of what doesn't—but you don't, and we here at your side are pleased
to have you with us, supposing that we'll make the way together.

NOTHING

. . . no evil thing is evil insofar as it exists,
but insofar as it is turned . . .
—Saint Gregory Palamás

What had I meant to say? Just now. I have forgotten.

    Which among our extant flourishing phenomena

        are you? Is that a limp? The evening drifts

into its routine dimming of particulars, quite

    literally *evening* the scene along the shore.

        We're all made even now, though you're still limping.

The little boats at anchor have retained a single stroke

    of gold to edge their canvas canopies, lent them

        by the setting sun's last flare. Their painted hulls

have all gone grey—if variously grey—and we

    are strolling the grey pavement to our suppers

        at the beach café—*το ψάροταβερνα*, we like to say.

I'm hoping for grilled octopus *με τζατζίκι,*

    παρακαλώ. Και μία μπίρα. Do you suppose

        those lights ahead might frame our destination for the night?

I think they might. We'll reach them soon enough and, when we have,

    we'll see with both our rods and cones and suddenly

        our colors will return. Meantime, have you noticed how

our evening stroll compels our taking pains attending

    to the variegated shade in hopes of stepping clear

        of ruts along the grey? None of them is adequately

evident amid continued dimming—which has of late

    become so nearly palpable that one could almost

        take it or mistake it for something of itself.

το ψάροταβερνα — to psárotaverna — the fishtavern
με τζατζίκι,παρακαλώ. Και μία μπίρα — meh tzatzeékee, parakalló. Keh meéuh beéruh
— with yogurt sauce, please. And a beer.

IDIOT PSALM 2

—a psalm of Isaak, accompanied by baying hounds

O Shaper of varicolored clay and cellulose, O Keeper

    of same, O Subtle Tweaker, Agent

    of energies both appalling and unobserved,

    do not allow Your servant's limbs to stiffen

    or to ossify unduly, do not compel Your servant

    to go brittle, neither cramping at the heart,

    nor narrowing his affective sympathies

    neither of the flesh nor of the allegéd soul.

Keep me sufficiently limber that I might continue

    to enjoy my morning run among the lilies

    and the rowdy waterfowl, that I might

    delight in this and every evening's intercourse

    with the woman You have set beside me.

Make me to awaken daily with a willingness

    to roll out readily, accompanied

    by grateful smirk, a giddy joy,

    the idiot's undying expectation,

    despite the evidence.

PURE ENOUGH

And if the tribal dialect has yet to be
sufficiently restored,

and if the pique and pallor of the public
discourse yet continues

to obscure and to efface without the merest
tremor of chagrin, one

might nonetheless resolve to hold the line within,
whenever possible

among one's also wincing cohort, honoring
the latent beauty of

the true, or, short of truth, what might of our troubled
moment pass for it.

ASPECT

The spirit's simulacra have obtained
    a spinning countenance both manifold
and manifest. And, lo, the spirit bides

within its every avatar unchanged,
    and, lo, the simulacra swerve beyond
appearances alone, but keep their deep

entirety composed in every face.
    You're dizzy? Just as well. Your dizziness
proves seemly here, up close, and cultivates

at last a sweet, uncommon modesty.

How long has glib presumption kept us both
unschooled and pleased with our elaborate

unschooling? No? How might you now suspect
    the spirit's effervescent quickening?
And I? I couldn't easily say, but might suppose

this sudden bubbling near the heart is meet
    and right, and promises one day to rise
to serve an altogether animate occasion.

LENTEN COMPLAINT

The breakfast was adequate, the fast
itself sub-par. We gluttons, having
modified our habits only somewhat
within the looming Lenten dark, failed
quite to shake our thick despair, an air
that clamped the heart, made moot the prayer.
As dim disciples having seen the light,
we supplied to it an unrelenting gloom.

Wipe your chin. I'm dying here
in Omaha, amid the flat, surrounded
by the beefy, land-locked generations,
the river, and the river's rancid shore.

O what I wouldn't give for a lifting,
cool salt breeze, a beach, a Labrador.

LATE HABIT

Prayer, he now supposed, was possible—if
manifestly intermittent—and on occasion
he felt as if he dreamt his prayer.

On rarest moments, the prayer had come
to speak itself, and he, in dim effusion,
took some care to listen as he spoke.

Offenses still occurred—the odd rebuff,
the snub, the petulant and prideful pout,
ubiquitous self-interest—but all had lately

become far more entertaining than offensive.
And those who bore no love for him became
the objects of his most tender turns of phrase.

Progress being, after all, at best incremental,
and the way ahead insistent in its endlessness,
a sudden calm had come to visit him, assuring

that the world he spoke and made partook of what
was actual, what lay poised beyond his ken,
and that such words would open ever and again.

IDIOT PSALM 3

—a psalm of Isaak, whispered mid the Philistines

Master both invisible and notoriously
     slow to act, should You incline to fix
Your generous attentions for the moment
     to the narrow scene of this our appointed

tedium, should You—once our kindly

secretary has duly noted which of us

is feigning presence, and which excused, which unexcused,

You may be entertained to hear how much we find to say

about so little. Among these other mediocrities,

Your mediocre servant gets a glimpse of how

his slow and meager worship might appear

from where You endlessly attend our dreariness.

Holy One, forgive, forgo and, if You will, fend off

from this my heart the sense that I am drowning here

amid the motions, the discussions, the several

questions endlessly recast, our paper ballots.

THE FRAGILE SURROUND

Availing space in which we live and move,

and chance to glimpse the trembling import of

our late, suspected being—and, well, yes,

the opening occasion of a guess

that, when we're after meaning, more is always

likelier to please than the common taste

of less with which our eager suppositions

are in the main rewarded. I'm thinking such

lacunae as this cove may lend us all their

latent agency each and every time

we enter, willing to attend the puzzle,

leaning in to ambiguity, aloof

to any fear accompanying what bit

we witness in the local, endless, fraught

fragility of every passing scene.

Keep up. I, too, had chance occasion, once,
to lean, to choose between two such modes of travel—
      that of knowing, clearly, what I meant to see
      and, on the other hand, not so sure, but eager
for the roads' divergences to obtain
to something skirting lumination.
      If I sigh now, it's not so much for me
      as for the prospect of a road constructed
as we go, bearing both our burdens and
ourselves, always just ahead, and bearing on.

And sure, we're hoping to proceed, to *get*
somewhere, and much of our attention speeds ahead.
      My point, I now suppose, has more to do
      with honoring the road itself, the ragged,
dust-glazed bracken by the side, and giving
each attendant host its due—the roebuck,
      woodchuck, turtle, and the toad, the hawk
      the raucous jay or raven yammering,
the fleet and near-angelic wren and chickadee,
the modest beetle, humble bee, blind ant.

SOMNAMBULANT

Every so often, I awaken and find
the world both vivid and lit, each element
—far as I can tell—lit from within. And yes,
like you, I may have assumed this radiance
to be a trick of morning sun upon the sea,
or the fortunate effect of ambient or
of manufactured light, of dumb or less
dumb luck. What I should now make clear
is that this intermittent waking is not
quite so literal as you are supposing, nor
so mundane; in fact, I may have been jogging, or
yammering on before a yawning class,
writing something or other on the blackboard.
I may have appeared more or less awake
right along, but suddenly, with little warning, I become
for the moment more fully awake, and I see
that there—along the path, among the bracken
or the pine, or even there, just now opening
within each forlorn face before me—a glistening,
a quality, a presence of light so profound
I can't but close my eyes to see.

IDIOT PSALM 4

—a psalm of Isaak, barely spoken

If I had anything approaching

      a new song, surely I would sing.

If I had sufficient vision,

      I would see.

If, amid the dim and dissolution

      of the January day, new music

      might avail to warm what passes

      for my heart, surely I would weep.

My enemies are plentiful, and I

      surround them, these enemies

      camped firmly in my heart, what passes,

      lo these dreary ages, for my heart.

O Lord of Hosts, do slay them.

II.
Hesychastérion

I beg you, never disregard a single soul,
especially when it happens to be a monk or a beggar.
For Your Charity knows that His place is among the beggars . . .

—*Saint Simeon of Syria, the Holy Fool*

LONG HABIT

I keep things metaphorical,
      and in so doing hope to keep
anxiety at bay, to keep
      my hold of fretwork neatly stowed
off shore in my precious little
      painted boat. *Yo! Estivador!*
Stuff the goods and keep them stuffed!

The sea, of course, is not so much
      inclined to mind our purposes,
and so the sea will of occasion
      skip the boats like flat stones back to shore.
What's more, the glib abyss will surely
      vent its bitter breath as well to dress
in froth the shore entirely.

How might this *figure*? And just what,
        if anything, is one obliged
to make of it? That every
        venture fronts resisting wind? That
every pilgrim idiot simply
        by setting out will also risk
such battering as my precious little boat?

HESYCHASTÉRION

I am etching out a dwelling   in the granite of my heart.
I am thinking then to torch   its walls and sweep out all debris
with a green, a heavy branch   of rosemary.

I mean to carve a niche inside   therein to rest a lamp,
and set behind that vigil lamp   an icon of the Christ,
and, kneeling there, lean in to find   a little taste

of stillness—that I might descend   full unto a likely depth
of vision and a whelming calm,   wherein I might obtain
an aspect likely as His own   and without stain.

I will prepare a censer—one   glowing coal, deep red amid
the heart's obscurity.   And leaning into what bides there
will place on it, mid-prayer,   a bit of myrrh.

Should I make my way at last   to the hollow of my heart,
I hope as well to apprehend   a stilling of the crowd,
within which stillness I might dare   approach the cloud.

IDIOT PSALM 5

—a psalm of Isaak raised in unaccustomed stillness

With unclean lips, at least, and yea
      with unclean hands, encumbered heart,
      congested, lo these many years,
      with no small measure of regret,
      and sin's particulate debris,
with these and countless other dear
      impediments, I stoop to find
      my knees. And on occasion You,
      Whose dimly figured Face I dare
      pursue to searing clarity,
      have condescended, acquiesced
      to grant what little I might bear.

AND YET ANOTHER PAGE AND YET

1.

One's waking of itself obtains
      a rising and—one might say—a dazed,
          surprising glee at having met
within sleep's netherworld one's own
      dim-shadowed psyche, and survived.

One's walking soon thereafter well
      into the morning's modest glare
          proves—if all goes swimmingly—yet
further evidence of being
      obliquely well attended, proves

discreetly provident of one's

      invisible surround and all

            that hidden cloud now pressing. Such

hid crowd and its solicitous

      attention can thereafter vest

in every snag a prospect further

      gathering. The lapping shoreline

            lay with its habitual—one

might note—recurrent chord attending

      its late-set revision of the edge

by which one visits once again

      one's limits, next the bay. And I

            set off along its seam to see

just what, by new laborious

      revision, had been newly made.

2.

What I found were varied clumps—debris

      of purple kelp, the toddler's pail,

            some several plastic shovels,

the odd cork sandal, and the always

      unnerving scraps of this or that

ruined shorebird, the orange, failed

      armor of the lobster, picked clean

            by beak and animated grit.

What to make of this collision—

      of cluttered mind and cluttered shore?

3.

Of endless if particular

　　destruction, yet accompanied

　　　　by vast enormity and might,

I made no great conclusion, save

　　　　to shed my walking gear and swim.

ARTICULATION

What I have come to say is never quite

　　sufficient; what I have come to say falls

ever short, if reliably—my one,

　　my only certainty. This fact, for now,

can prove both deep discouragement and deep,

　　elusive hope. I've come to trust our words'

most modest crap shoot; I have come, as well,

　　to see their limit as my proof. If, one

fresh morning, I should come to apprehend

　　how ever full with presence every breath

now is—and even now—I have a sense

　　my words would grow so heavy as to still.

I suppose that morning then would open

　　to our eighth day, whose sunrise will not set.

—for Warren Farha

IDIOT PSALM 6

—a psalm of Isaak, hoarsely sung

And yet again the wicked in his arrogance,

    in his acutely hemmed and tapered sense

    of self has found

    sufficient opportunity to hound

    the lowly.

And yet again, Great Enabler, the lowly,

    draped in their accustomed modesty

    and threadbare suits bereft

    have seized the chance to suffer quietly, stage left.

Therefore, now again, I puzzle why,

    O Holy Silence, why

    do You appear to bide unheeding

    some great distance hence?

Why, O Blithely *Un*apparent, do you remain

    serenely imperceptible, even to our thinning

    crew who stand here blinking at the sky?

I have no stomach for the newspapers, no heart

    for the brilliant, lit flat-screen catalog

    of woes, though every item flickers,

    one admits, wondrously produced

    and duly sponsored.

See here. The wicked boasts about his late

    successes, the grasping man complains

    that he is cheated of his share, while all

    the while the self-concerned continue

    banking largely on Your accustomed reticence,

    and must needs let out their trousers still

    several measures more, having wagered well.

Pinched beneath their spinning machinations

    and all their neat machines,

    we grind our teeth,

    yea, even as we sleep.

TO WHAT MIGHT THIS BE COMPARED?

As one peering, fixed,

    into the icon's

        limpid eye observes

a subtle quickening,

    just there, beyond

        the opaque plane—

As one tugging up

    his socks and lacing

        sturdy boots to take

another season's

    turn around the Holy

        Mountain's desert span—

As one, crushed again

    by failed, flailing prayer,

        finds of a moment

and in the stillness

    of the cave a breath

        both cool and welcoming—

so I observed yet

    one more chance reprieve,

        shook my head, and rose.

TWO TREES

1.

Complicity is both
subtle and pervasive,
bears upon its branches
a latent taste of how
each apologetic
figure, thus encumbered,
might puzzle even now
at its brief occasion
dangling, and spun about
on one sere limb amid
a fraught complexity
of other drynesses.
Of our regrettable
and ancient grab for what
still passes hereabouts
as knowledge, and of its
bleak result accreting,
one finds in the debris
little compensation.
Puzzle or not, one might
happen on more likely
fruit by first admitting
to the mix one's own mute
involvement in the crime.
You there, in the mirror,
suppose we hunker down
to fix this sprawling mess,

or fix for once upon
a now more promising
appraisal of its reach.
For all we know, the end
of knowledge is simply
that we might glimpse how all
we're likely to admit
continues spinning well
beyond our ken. Instead
of whining about it,
we might savor its late
provision of reprieve
as an ever-looming
providence, within which
even the exile might
yet find a likely plot,
and take a God damned seat.

2.
Having tasted knowledge,
having found how thin, how
surprisingly bland both
the flavor and bouquet
of its spent nectars turn
on the collective tongue
—even if attended
by decay's peculiar,
cloying scent and promise—
we might move finally
to the second tree, long

abandoned, all but lost
to tribal memory.
Its living, life-availing
branches do not appear
to have suffered much by long
disinterested neglect.
Whether by wholesale chagrin,
subconscious habit, or
plain willfulness, we have
quite neatly pruned it from
the family narrative,
forgotten that it ever
grew so close at hand—
laden, available,
never once forbidden.
Whatever *good* or *evil*
have come to mean, they can
hardly account for what
it is I'm after now—
though all I'd ask at present
is some sense of purpose
and a steady pulse. Still
overlooked, the still
bright tree does liven up
the garden, bears—even
now—its unfamiliar fruit,
stands to quicken any
would care to eat of it,
should she so much as deign
to lift a blesséd hand.

MYSTAGÓGIA

He came then to believe that what he wrote
was true, that poring over what he wrote
revealed, now and then again, another
glimpse of promise in the simple—the sometimes
not so simple—words he wrote. That others
had long since given up attending to
the ancient, inexpressive chore no longer
troubled him, nor troubled the cool, bright air
holding still, still holding as a fragrant
cove above, around, within the lighted page.
He wrote then to observe what he believed,
to find within that cove a place to breathe.

IDIOT PSALM 7

—a psalm of Isaak, pled

And lo, the fraught perplexities accrue,
      collude, compound, and hasten to compose
      before us now and, yea, extending far
      as we might squint into the distance.

No, more likely they turn witless, mute,
      and we become about as sentient and as
      adept as any stump decaying in a feedlot.

Meantime, yes, perplexities accrue.
      The aging Labrador's stiff leg won't
      let her climb the stair. Our neighbor's late
      C-section has brought fresh heartbreak home.

I swear the very air smells of tar or creosote, maybe

tire rubber burning. The game ball's rolled

clean off the court. A little help!

KOL NIDRE

Good to reconsider, and then to disavow

whatever mitigations one has let usurp,

eclipse, or glibly water down whatever good

he may have thought to offer. Some untoward something

will often sprout from any swollen hull thus sown.

The unforeseen is guaranteed to flourish well

beyond the harried terms of any vow expressed

from one's more narrow sense or solitary will.

Good therefore to have another go at what

might prove of use beyond one's dim intention, no?

Good thereafter to unsay, recant what harm

has billowed, subsequent, from ill-considered

promise. Good that one prepare ever to repent.

III.
My Byzantium

. . . let him become a fool, that he may be wise.

—Saint Paul to the Colossians

IDIOT PSALM 8
—a Psalm of Isaak, winced

For, lo, our backs are prone
   to slow degeneration;
   our stiffened shoulders
   ache with every effort,
   our knees are fairly shot.

The boggled mind
   goes numb, more numb
   it seems with every season
   borne beneath such weathers,
   every wind. Our poor,
   recurrent thoughts turn
   circling, if increasingly
   imprecise. The earth itself
   inclines to tremble with what
   seems deep despair, while yea,
   the heavens positively
   glare in frank disdain.

Hobbled by broad ignorance and no less

hobbled by vast evidence,

one limps along the limen

longing to be whole,

and—if You will—to cross.

SPECULATION ALONG THE WAY

The roaring alongside he takes for granted . . .
—from "Sandpiper" by Elizabeth Bishop

When of a given evening, say, an evening

    laced with storm clouds skirting distance parsed

by slanting light, or when the thickening air

    of an August afternoon by the late approach

of just such a storm turns suddenly thin and cool,

    and the familiar roaring for the moment made

especially unmistakable by distant thunder may

    seem oddly to be answered from within—that's how it

feels, anyway—and when, of a moment, that roaring

    couples as well with sudden calm—interior, exterior, it

hardly matters—in *that* fortunate incursion whereby

    the roar itself is suddenly interred, you

might startle to having had a taste of what

    will pass as prayer, or a taste, at the very least, of how

fraught, how laden the visible is, even

    as you work to find a likely figure for its uncanny

agency. Sure, I'm making this up as I go, hoping—even

as I go—to be finally getting somewhere. And maybe I am.

Maybe I'm taking you along. Let's say it's so, and say

however late the hour we now commence.

WINTERTIME AGORA: SALONIKA

You haven't very much to fear,

have little left to shirk, though each

of us must feel (I know I do)

a little like these bluing perch

laid out beside the mackerel.

The way they're pressed into the ice—

and look! the way they steam, transfixed

in interlacing strata, fronts

a very nearly sculptural

design. Sure, it starts to be

a little scary. And the crisp

salt scent of all their kind pervades

our packed *agora*, laced of course

with countless other odors, spiced

with intermittent, raw *ennui*.

See, it isn't exactly fear.

More a troubled melancholy

at the sight, maybe at the press,

of so many icebound species

and of so many similarly

steaming strangers packed into

a bleak, oppressed proximity.
> The thought of our last summer here
>> keeps tugging at my sleeve, when I

and my daughter inched slowly through
> this very spot, led—I now recall—
>> by my wife and son likewise

parting the waters just ahead.
> Hard to gather fully how time
>> and weather and the aching lack

of kin have worked the common scene
> into so fraught a circumstance.
>> The olives, fish, the various

hanging meats provide a jumbled
> figure for an also jumbled
>> disposition as I move

alone regardless, and so slowly
> with the crowd whose breath has filled
>> the packed agora like a cloud.

HEAVENLY CITY (*OURANOÚPOLI*)

The boats are not so Byzantine as practical,
small and narrow, bearing but one man to a skiff.

They are neither golden nor enameled
but they are very pretty just the same.

The old men manning most of them speak constantly,
even when alone, and, just now, this one mends

a far too-frail-seeming fishnet, shuttling
the oiled, wooden pin in a very practiced

manner, miraculously borne by fingers
looking very like queer, flexible cigars.

I pause here to prepare my entry to
the Holy Mountain, and I often stop here

for some days on my return. The octopus
at the beach café is nicely done,

and matched with beer and yogurt makes a hearty
welcome back. The world remains a puzzle,

no matter how many weeks one stands
apart from it, no matter how one tries

to see its troubled surfaces, or hopes
to dip beneath them for a glimpse of what it is

that makes this all appear to tremble so.

SLOW BOAT TO BYZANTIUM
—Ouranoúpoli, 2009

Just west of heaven's city, the aging,
    and disheveled *Áxion Estín*
        lies anchored in a shallow cove and far

as I can tell will not be hauling us
    to our famous Holy Mountain anytime soon.
        Country for old men, the uncommonly

wise, or—you may note—the sorely wounded young,

    Mount Athos reaches its green slope and dazzling

        granite far into the calm Aegean's blue.

Slow pilgrims of our middling generation

    may also find brief and random refuge there

        —so long as we find ourselves another boat.

As if on cue, the *Saint Panteleímon*

    shudders into view and beats a hulking,

        churning line to make the pier with time to spare.

And so, we scurry to the deck, submit

    to have our papers checked, and climb the iron stairs

        to stow our packs beneath the iron benches.

If any of this frank, confusing clatter

    has distracted you from prayer, the odds are good

        the whole endeavor is already somewhat

compromised. Take heart. These ups and downs will not

    abate, so you will surely find in time

        a practice less dependent on good fortune.

IDIOT PSALM 9

—a Psalm of Isaak, in the stillness

We say *flight of the imagination*,
but stand ankle deep in silt. We say *deep
life of the mind*, but seal the stone to keep
the tomb untouched. O Stillness. Nearly all
we find to say we speak for the most part
unawares, what little bit we think to say
unmoved, O Great Enormity Unmoved.

Brief thaw turned ragged March extending, O
Lost Cause, into yet another ragged April, *so.*
Brief shoots of new green trampled underfoot
by sleet, and lo, accumulating weather, moot,
sore-clipped—spring flowers tattered with the cold.

Lord, we say, *have mercy on us*, by which
each idiot more nearly means to plead
O Silent One Unspeaking, save me.

APPROACHING THE HOLY MOUNTAIN

—Ágion Óros, 15 December, 2007

Although a common winter chill
    has slowed us all this morning,
        and while the boat's enormity

huddles at the pier, so manifestly
    disinclined to move, one might
        just the same observe a subtle

quickening here. The air is traced
    by wood smoke, and the sea
        lies motionless and flat,

taking in a flurried, frail
    snowfall unimpressed. The gulls
        and terns are few and oddly

hushed. The crew, both bleary-eyed,
    and slow, proves surprisingly
        polite; and, as I say, for all

the chill, the weight of sudden

      stillness, a firm if pulsing heat

            has found again the tender

hollow near the heart, and this

      isn't just the coffee talking, nor

            the *τσίπουρο*. Sure, lean ahead

and hope to glimpse the green expanse

      out there along the sea (both lately

            patched with snow). In two hours' time,

the boat will fetch us to an also

      snowbound port, where we'll commence

      a season wrested somewhat

out of time—not to say that

      we are altogether ready,

         just slightly more prepared.

τσίπουρο — tseépooro — Greek grappa

TO SAY SILENCE
—Móni Xenofóndos, December, 2010

As the wind at last relented, I had meant

      in all earnest to say *silence*, but silence

wouldn't quite obtain, nor would any late felt

absence indicate the depth of sudden

      focus undisturbed, whether by abatement

of chattering leaves or of the high pitched

whistling of wild weather through the weathered gate.

       I'm saying as the wind let up, what I met
was more a profound quieting, if one

that nonetheless resounds. A pulse, and full, and
       very full. And yes, I know how foolish this
will seem. For all the endless yammering that fills

my head most waking moments and so often
       pulls me up from sleep, or draws me puzzling far
and suddenly away from the roiling confusion that most

often complicates my sleep, I find—now and
       again and profoundly—of one rare morning
a sudden hush, an emptying, and find

       my poor attention seize, grow heavy, then light.

EREMITE

—Katounákia, 2007

The cave itself is pleasantly austere,
       with little clutter—nothing save
a narrow slab, a threadbare woolen wrap,
       and in the chipped out recess here
three sooty icons lit by oil lamp.
       Just beyond the dim cave's aperture,
a blackened kettle rests among the coals,
       whereby, each afternoon, a grip
of wild greens is boiled to a tender mess.
       The eremite lies prostrate near

two books—a gospel and the Syrian's
    collected prose—whose pages turn
assisted by a breeze. Besides the thread
    of wood smoke rising from the coals,
no other motion takes the eye. The old
    man's face is pressed into the earth,
his body stretched as if to reach ahead.
    The pot boils dry. He feeds on what
we do not see, and may be satisfied.

DAWN AT SAINT ANNA'S SKETE

—Ágion Óros, 2006

The air is cool and is right thick with birdsong
as our bleary crew files out, of a sudden
disinterred from three sepulchral hours of prayer
into an amber brilliance rioting
outside the cemetery chapel. With bits
of Greek and English intermixed, the monks
invite us to the portico for coffee,
παξιμάδια, a shot of cold ρακί.
As I say, the air is cool, animate
and lit, and in such light the road already
beckons, so I skip the coffee, pound the shot,
and pocket two hard biscuits. And yes, the way
is broad at first, but narrows soon enough.

παξιμάδια — pahximáthia — Greek biscotti
ρακί — rahkeé— another name for τσίπουρο, Greek grappa

IDIOT PSALM 10

*—a psalm of Isaak, breathed beneath the chirp of
evening swallows*

O Hidden Hand upholding

    all wrought works now

    flourishing before us, O

    Mad Architect of exuberant

    abundance, of flora both sweet

    and acrid, and lo, of all furred fauna

    frolicking the field, both the mild

    and the less so, baring tooth

    and claw and, lo, so often

    leaving in their wake so many

    tufts of plumage, tattered fur.

O Great Zookeeper attending all such

    critters in Your ken, both microscopic

    and immense, the countless

    little fishes, our dear array

    of water mammals, yea, and this

    our great and lumbering leviathan

    fathoms deep, invisible.

O Most Secret Agent of our numberless

    occasions, please also mitigate

    the ache attending all of the above.

IV.
Erotic Word

One might well become a holy fool oneself here!
It's catching!

—*Razkolnikov, from* Crime and Punishment

∽

. . . *"do not weep, life is paradise, and we are all in paradise,*
but we do not know it, and if we did want to know it,
tomorrow there would be paradise the world over."
—*Markel, the elder brother of Father Zosimas, from* The Brothers
Karamazov

IDIOT PSALM 11
—a psalm of Isaak, growled against the floorboards

O Undisclosed, O Surreptitious, O Most
    Furtive Father of all things manifest
    and all things tucked away, O Pulse
    Unceasing within each quark, both
    up and down, both strange and charm, O
    Deep Threefold Only Who sets amid this
    vast menagerie Your pouting children, we
    who for some duration remain, oddly

propelled and for the most part upright,

if alternately weeping, if alternately

bursting forth in broad guffaw, O Arch

and Covert Cause do come again, incline

yet to be shown here in our midst, You

Who Are, allegedly, ever here, and ever

thus, impossibly among us.

EX ORIENTE LUX

As morning light reorients the eye

    and undertakes to woo the pilgrim's gaze

slightly farther to the east, just so

    the latent blaze beneath the heart obtains

the fortunate illusion of a pulse

    now answering the elemental rays.

DRAW NEAR

—προσέλθετε

For near is where you'll meet what you have wandered

far to find. And near is where you'll very likely see

how far the near obtains. In the dark *καθόλικον*

the lighted candles lent their gold to give the eye

a more than common sense of what lay flickering

just beyond the ken, and lent the mind a likely

swoon just shy of apprehension. It was then

that time's neat artifice fell in and made for us

a figure for when time would slip free altogether.

I have no sense of what this means to you, so little

sense of what to make of it myself, save one lit glimpse

of how we live and move, a more expansive sense in Whom.

προσέλθετε — prosélthehteh — draw near
καθόλικον — kathóleekon — the central church of a monastery

ODE: EROTIC WORD

O dark shivering in the roots and the leaves!
—Seferis, from "Erotikos Logos"

1.

So like a petal the fragrant   areole dimpling here

at the tip of the tongue, and yes   so like a bud blossoming

is the willing response. Eros   thus awakened also

bids the bodies draw to reach   their meet, agreeable repose,

gathering an ache and urgency   into the lush escape

from clarity unto a far   more promising confusion.

And yes, so like that sacramental   idiom the murmured

course of lip and touch and taste   compounding, drawing two to take

the heady liquor of this   communal cup, flowing, its flower

bearing fruit and fragrance toward   the sudden speech of two as one.

2.

Of all our meet occasions, this

becomes us most, and undertakes

to keep us thus: most becoming,

most engaged, most attentive to

the mystery engraved in this

our common body, blessed with both

the pulse of animality

and Spirit's animating breath.

And look, we witness yet a third

appealing aspect of our kind;

we startle to observe how far

more nearly home we are when joined.

3.

I was lost without her. And, over time, we have been lost together

at dim intervals, when this or that drew our saving, rapt attention

away from the mystery we held, away from the immediacy

of its fruit—our children and this our love and this our thus awakened

disposition to attend to *every* other from that sacred place our meeting

bore and bears. Repentance is never fit if the turn is nothing but *away*

from one regrettable occasion or singeing grief; its purpose and sole

agency depend—in thought and act and word—upon the turning *to*,

which is what I mean to say to her just now, and saying hope to serve.

IDIOT PSALM 12

—a psalm of Isaak, amid uncommon darkness

O Being both far distant and most near,

O Lover embracing all unlovable, O Tender

Tether binding us together, and binding, yea

and tenderly, Your Person to ourselves,

Being both beyond our ken, and kindred, One

Whose dire energies invest such clay as ours

with patent animation, O Secret One secreting

life anew into our every tissue moribund,

afresh unto our stale and stalling craft,

grant in this obscurity a little light.

ERATO'S INSTRUCTION

I like that you worry every word, she said.
It reminds me of myself. She took my hand
and brushed it with her lips. *And I am*

specially pleased to know you test each tender
phoneme with your tongue—and so thoroughly.
She brought her lips to mine, still whispering,

and most of all, I find your willingness
to learn, well, irresistible, so much so
that it surprises even me. Her sudden breath

met mine in what was then a lively coupling,
a likely give and take. *And see*, she breathed,
as two are brought together they educe

a novel third—as we addressed the matter
of the moment to accommodate a due
confusion of invention and intent.

Discovery, she breathed into my ear,
depends on just such willingness, a faith
in what may come of one's surrendering

the meager expectations, and a hope
that what another brings to the affair
is worth the trouble.

LATE INCARNATION

In her sleep she must have said aloud and he
rising to her darkened surface just
in time to hear
the troubled air that followed what it was
she must have said.

The August heat that held the room then also
wrought his waking—so hungry for
the press of her
his throat both ached and pulsed. And leaning
fully into her he met the hum of what
she must have said.

IDIOT PSALM 13

—Isaak's penitential psalm, unaccompanied

Again, and yes again, O Ceaseless Tolerator
    of our bleaking recurrences, O Forever Forgoing
    Forgone (*sans* conclusion), O Inexhaustible,
    I find my face against the floor, and yet again
    my plea escapes from unclean lips, and from a heart
    caked in, constricted by its own soiled residue.
You are forever, and forever blessed, and I aspire

one day to slip my knot and change things up,

to manage at least one late season sinlessly,

to bow before You yet one time without chagrin.

EROTIKOS LOGOS

I like very much how you lean just now

      clean into the book, beginning the day

in such charitable expectation.

      I like how you are so nearly smiling.

I almost see it—and your eyes seeming

      lit from within. We, all of us, have been

disappointed in the past. Already

      I fear your being disappointed now.

So much, of course, depends upon your own

      willingness to find something worthy here,

even as you bring—as you must—something

      worthy to the effort. So much of what

is worthy wants always two struggling toward

      agreeable repose, requires grateful

coupling of a willing one with an also

      willing other. I would like for us to find

again the faculty to apprehend

      this eros honestly, and so to find

a way to meet in eros a likely

      figure for most of what we do worth doing.

WHEN I SAY *I ACHE FOR YOU*

First, though, I should make clear that when I say
I love you I admit a deep confusion figuring
a mix of selfish joys and gratitude, and if
I say *you are my life* such talk would also prove
both broadly vexed and gesturing in evermore
elusive trope with weak abstraction dimming
the horizon. Early on, startling to the fact of you
then waking in my sleep-slow arms I'm sure I said
you have made me better than I was—whatever
that has come to mean by now. But when I say
I ache for you I am not speaking metaphorically,
as every figuration quiets to this moment,
mute, which absolutely aches, as if the heart
had risen from its roaring cave to press
with sudden heat and weight, low in the throat,
an absolutely animal occasion where
the pulse with all its music meets the breath, just here.

—for Marcia

EROTIKOS LOGOS II

Eros is our agency,
      logos our lit word
implicating yet one more
      bright latency—and here,
and oddly calm amid such
      roiling surge as this,

as any, salt-strewn moment,

as this, as any,

coupled two composing of

their gleaming bodies one

thus luminous occasion.

ANNUNCIATION

Deep within the clay, and O my people
very deep within the wholly earthen
compound of our kind arrives of one clear,
star-illumined evening a spark igniting
once again the tender of our lately
banked noetic fire. She burns but she
is not consumed. The dew lights gently,
suffusing the pure fleece. The wall comes down.
And—*do you feel the pulse?*—we all become
the kindled kindred of a king whose birth
thereafter bears to all a bright nativity.

IDIOT PSALM 14

—a psalm of Isaak, sore afraid

Μετά φόβου Θεού, πίστεως καί αγάπης, προσέλθετε.

Forgive, O Fire, forgive, O Light, the patent,
fraught impurity of we who thus presume
to open unclean lips, availing now
a portal for Your purity. Forgive
the chatter of our blithely fearless crowd

awaiting Your pure body pretty much

the way we stand in any fast-food queue,

considering our neighbors' faults, puzzling

at those odd few who seem to shiver some

as they approach Your wound. Holy One allow

that as we near the cup, before the coal

is set upon our trembling tongues, before

we blithely turn and walk again into

our many other failures, allow that we

might glimpse, might apprehend something of the fear

with which we should attend this sacrifice,

for which we shall not ever be found worthy,

for which—I gather—we shall never be prepared.

Μετά φόβου Θεού, πίστεως καί αγάπης, προσέλθετε — metáh fóvoo
Theoó, peéstehos keh agápees, prosélthehteh — With the fear of
God, faith and love, draw near.

JUVENILIA AND UNCOLLECTED POEMS

GOOD-NIGHT

Before you paint his portrait
find a good thick brush   camel hair
Think hard   His face   The eyes   Now
one generous splash on top
and on each side-post   There
We're safe   Good-night

(1974)

EVOCATION

Imagine her asleep,
on her side, facing away
with one arm falling
behind.

She is not so pure
as white wool,
nor
is she so soft
as grass.
(She is not green.)
This woman is no poem, though
close.

Remember her
breath (that close),
her shoulders, rounded;
remember
her breasts, and
sleep.

(1976)

VISITOR

This man visits me often
in my apartment near the park.
When he comes by, he tells stories sure
to break his heart, not mine. Then, oddly,
he giggles like a child, his white head
bobbing, and after a time signals the end
of his visit with a sudden silence
that folds him in.

From my high window
I can see him in the park, his elbows bent
to his knees. As if early for some
appointment, he leans forward
in his bench, his right side
pressed against the armrest.

Some time ago, his right eye
turned in, settled for sleep
like a tired dog. He has fashioned
a corduroy patch so children
won't be frightened.

(1976)

A GRANDFATHER'S PASSING

I want you to see him
as he was, those last days:

His skin pulled tight
against the high bones
of his face; his eyes, huge
and urgent; he could not talk.

One of the early strokes had stolen
his voice, and, in the end, when he tried
to write to us, only he knew
what those odd marks meant.

(1976)

CAMEL SEQUENCE

1.
Before you do so much as
melt butter in the pan, decide—
do you really want to cook this camel?

2.
It is rumored that there are some
camels without much hump. Instead,
their feet fill up, creating
an entirely new beast: an obviously
well-balanced quadri-ped,
whose movement sounds
not unlike a river, or
your stomach when it's watery, or,
for that matter, a regular camel.

3.

[Filler: ad libitum. *Note: any mention*
of camels shall be considered
unintentional]

An eagle flies. An orca
also, briefly, flies.
There are some things with which
a poem cannot compare:

> the positions of the sun,
>
> an evening light,
>
> a woman's breast,
>
> her thighs.

The simple thought of these
stirs me like
camels.

(1976)

SOUTH AMERICAN SEQUENCE

1.

In terms
of utility, a man's
most valuable tool
is his machete.

2.

Everyone in the club
is watching
the moisture at the hip
of Carmen's left leg.

3.

Father to son: *Make
your machete sing!*

4.

Father to son: Brood
over coffee dark seas.

5.

Argentine beef.

6.

Mother to daughter: *Make
his machete sing!*

(1976)

WOLF HUNT

His breathing, shallow
like light wind, a Lummi boy waits
above the mud trail, hugging his perch
in an old alder.

And you
finally come, weary
from a three day hunt
without success.
Your mind is thick and slow with hunger,
or you would know to turn and run.

It is good you are so hungry, you
are barely conscious; you do not feel
the alder spear snap your neck.

(1977)

PUGET SOUND WINTER

This is where we live—the smoky gap
between ranges, the dim instant
of memory, the sudden click between fingers.

These are the spaces we fill and are made
to fill. It is only fit
that we settle in, decorate

what livable space these lowlands afford
with eyes open for the break
of color when it comes.

(1977)

INTRODUCTION

To begin with
his straw hat has come apart
in the back and rests low
on his head. He carries it there
with a careful,
steady step that seems
to bend him into an older man.

Look hard, and see him; he's here
just ahead of you. There's little you can do
to avoid him.

(1977)

OR HAVE LEFT ME

You are dead, or
have left me; I can't remember which.
I do know that I sit alone, that I
have ten strange fingers, and that something whistles
in my lungs. Odd, the way a face can hang so
heavily, and can seem to pull an entire body down.

If a hand were to change, become something
altogether different, say, a grip of flowers, or
a club of dirt, one might understand the strangeness,
might say out loud, *There, that's the problem;*
something's changed my hand to dirt.

(1978)

A LETTER
—for Fred Eckman

I wanted to say
something to you
of Golgotha, and perhaps
find some word or other
to explain a world
that would allow

such a stone. Some hand
unseen took the apology
from me before I
knew, and left us
only with this dim planet
and that old rock
grinning in its shadow.

(1978)

THE DIGGINGS

We do not leave
the Ozette beach behind.
There is nothing
stays behind for very long.
So I recall the light
of a winter storm
on longhouses, the light
on a stand of dwarf madrona.
I would recall women
pounding mussels into something
their children might eat.
I would remember
brown dogs nosing the dirt,
tossing through the shells
of the insignificant dead.

(1979)

HERE

a burst of iris so that . . .
—William Carlos Williams

Here among grasses
I find you, perhaps asleep, lying
deeply among grasses. In the air
a warm odor of cows and mown
grass. And in the air something
equally warm, an odor very
like the grass but not.

I might stoop to wake you, sit
to discuss the real things, cows
and dirt, the embrace of deep grasses.

But your sleep (if it is sleep) keeps me
standing away. And the shape of you
lying among grasses is one
I would not change.

(1979)

YOU SAY *KALALOCH*

(ka LAY lok)

You say *Kalaloch*, and the word
holds your tongue like a lover. You know
the chafe of sand, the rough touch
of north wind. Whole years
would discover you still wandering this beach,
a woman in rags, and only a little mad.

Was it here I found the raven, here
the swollen dog?
The tiny black snails
are good to eat; you can boil them
in a coffee pot, pluck them steaming
from their shells, taste the sea rising
in the meat. You know this place, have grown
familiar with its taste, its salt
smell. You have brushed its sand
from your wet body, rubbed sand
from your brown skin. Even as you
turn away, you carry Kalaloch in your hair.

(1980)

ROADKILL

Before us, this road
through a U.S. forest, its
darkness kept by high timber
along either side. It is a black
oil tar road, and all
along it—the gathered heath
of lichen and fern, the caught
breath of mosses. Here, something
moans for the insignificant,
mourns the insignificant dead.

(1980)

SO WE ARE CAUGHT HERE

as if each morning were a waking
to the shock of wind off the bay
and all the whining of sea birds
held the quick alarm of human calling.

I've seen those birds, and heard
their crying through the thick morning
of the bay; I've imagined women
frantic through the fog, their white arms

tearing through the fog's white wall
to find somewhere in the water a few yards out,
the child asleep beyond waking, rocked
in the sure grip of the hidden bay.

(1981)

NATURE TALK

Sit back and listen.
It's time the lesson
were taken up again,
here, surrounded
by the easy talk
of trees and wind,
the hard fact of rock
pushed up through rich soil.

The lesson then: Rabbits
are as prolific here as anywhere,
and porcupines—if not overly
abundant—reliably keep the world
in porcupines. Muskrats, I am told,
have, up close, an odor tolerable
only to other muskrats, and skunks,
despite themselves, happily increase.

(1981)

BACK THEN TO A TIME

when there was less difference
between you and a deer
than now between you and me:
If we were unhappy, we
simply changed our tune, fell in
to what it was the day required.
And if for some reason we wanted
to see in darkness, we closed our eyes
so that somewhere inside
the light blinked on to show us
what we wanted. Still, given
what we have come to call
the world, we might expect
a little erosion.
                    Here and now,
all gaps grow wider, you and I
will never meet, and the deer

will have nothing to do with us.
Simple light is hard enough
to come by, and distance
darkens, looms unchecked.

—*for William Stafford*

(1981)

PASSION

It's the simple difference
between the ways you love
one man or woman and the ways
you love the others. So let's have
no more talk of its being
a somehow lesser thing;
it carries with it all
those other shades of affection
and gives them whatever
extra taste for goodness
it is that lets you
take your lover's toe
to you mouth, being glad
for any pleasure such a thing
might give her.

(1983)

REVISITING

All day, something missing
or confused—as I helped my mother
slice onions, as I took in the game
on t.v. with my dad, even
as the evening slowed us, first
into familiar conversation, then
as we sank lost into a kind of sleep
reviewing the confusion of photos
in the album, from each of them
a boy smiling at our dream.

              And now
waking very early to find my wife
sleeping beside me in that boy's bed—
the emptiness of that room so startling
I have to sit up to calm myself.
Somewhere, deeper in the house, my parents
are curled together in their sleep. Outside,
a dog limps across the lawn, his nose
glancing a lost scent that insists
on pulling him along. It is still
very early, and still very dark,
but I dress to go outside, and I hurry.
Somewhere beyond the gesture
of this house, my dog
is looking for me. I must
help him find me.

(1984)

HOW I LOST MY EYE

Nam. And I'm hunkered blind
in a stinking paddy, trying
to keep my head covered and trying
to open a tin can with my blade
when some pfc spills his grenade
three bodies down the line.

No. I'm pushing hard to fell
this tree before early snow and this darkening
slope shut down the work until spring
and leave me staring at the blank backyard
for months when the saw bucks hard
and the chain flies off the maul.

Listen. I'm fishing the Puyallup
high above the fork and looking
to hook some sockeye or king
just dumb enough to take
more than bait when my line
grabs rock, and pissed off I snap the rod up.

How's this: I'm buying groceries
at Honest Don's and looking for something
to stew with a load of chicken wings
or maybe this pale cut of ham
when the milk truck slams
into the storefront from the street.

OK, Dick. It didn't happen anything
like what I've said—just a long, dull pain
that didn't so much as make a sound, nothing

to give away the closing scene—just
my life, this ridiculous routine,
and the opportunity.

(1984)

FARMING THE SALT FLATS

Sure, we almost went broke, trying to coax
our crop of wilted lettuces from that
blanched dust; still, things *did* grow: flaccid carrots,

a sort of gum potato, row upon row
of our dreary, brown lettuces that flapped
like acres of rags in our constant wind.

All of that proved challenging. And it proved
challenging at first to move our produce
at market. Always, the same Philistine

complaint: lettuces, carrots, potatoes—
they all look so old!
Well, after some convincing, one or two

greengrocers agreed to a little taste,
after which, they could barely speak, but fell
to sudden reverie, troubled by a smile.

Once they had come upon such bitterness,
the citizens would not do without it,
demanded reliable supply.

Outlets have sprung up in every corner.
Distribution is now our sole concern,

parceling the yield without riot.

So hard to believe, all the years wasted
in sweet corn, when what the multitude craved
was a satisfying, tangible grief.

(1984)

WORDS FOR MY FATHER

And this is the consolation—that the world
doesn't end, that the world one day
opens up into something better, and that we
one day open up into something far better.
Maybe like this: one morning you finally wake
to a light you recognize as the light you've wanted
every morning that has come before. And the air
itself has some light thing in it that you've always
hoped the air might have. And one is there
to welcome you whose face you've looked for during all
the best and worst times of your life. He takes you to himself
and holds you close until you fully wake.

And it seems you've only just awakened, but you turn
and there we are, the rest of us, arriving just behind you.

We'll go the rest of the way together.

(1988)

MY TRAGIC EFFORTS

I am exhausted. I cannot focus.
I am driven to self-destructive thoughts.
Were it not for the richly flowered air
of Florianopolis to revive me
I would surely die.

Forgive my exaggeration—must be the heat.
I have been hiding my poems from the man
I dream, the pale man who cannot quite read.
Just the same, I have not been successful.
Success eludes me.

If anything, my care has made him more
cavalier with my poems, his translations.
So Cavalier! Raimundo, try harder.
Make a new poem, a poem he cannot change!
What would that be? A dead poem?

No, be satisfied with the various poem,
the acquiescent, bootlicking poem, the poem
so eager to please that it will become
anything, will lift its bed and walk! Thereafter,
able to travel the broad world, an agreeable
poem, willing to mirror any foolish
face caught looking.

(1989)

SUSCEPTIBILITIES

The child's face was heartbreaking, so I turned
the television off before my own
attentive daughter could see how ill
the girl was, before Elizabeth saw
what I had seen in the girl's dull eyes: vast

weariness, proximate death. I don't know.
I don't know. This sort of thing is ever
available no matter how many times
one turns off the news, or turns away
from whatever most recent token rises

to insist, albeit powerlessly, on some notice.
Well, I'd give *all* my attention
to the girl, or her brothers, or her frail,
oppressed people, if attention *did* anything.
But you don't need me to tell you how vain

attention proves alone, *and* good intentions, those
few earnest conversations we savor
with our black coffee after a big meal.
Awareness may prove nothing more or less
than complicity. So I keep turning

my daughter away from what goes on with
vengeance just one or two countries over,
or across town, or next door, or here
in my own numb heart. She's a bright, discerning
child, and she would ask too many questions.

(1989)

A RECUPERATION OF SIN
(EARLIER VERSION)

1.

I suppose the issue is less

what you call it—this recurring

tendency toward bad manners—

than a dim appeal to recourse.

Don't call it sin, if sin suggests

excuses, somehow diminished

culpability. In City

General, the tiny boy

lay all the more belittled

by the enormous bed and all

the beeping monitors that marked

his slow descent. In the county jail,

his dull parents waiting to learn

the extent of their crime, having

withheld food from their two boys

as a kind of lesson about behavior. Now,

one boy was under observation; one

was less than that. The dying son

would last another day or two.

His brother would survive, brain damaged

but of improving disposition.

2.

And I don't guess you'd call it sin
that Gaza's children musn't play
outside, or, for that matter, aren't
much safer staying in. And when
our clever, homemade bombs rained
on Baghdad, it wasn't sin exactly
that let them go. And sin didn't
necklace Soweto's less vicious
adolescents, nor tempt the acned
neo-Nazi thugs who met last
evening two doors down.

3.

Of war,
of war's savory rumor,
of war's speculative economics,
of the faithlessness that punches first,
of children lost, or thrown away, or worse,
of those without shelter, without food,
of blood spilled on wet tile

      or spilled on pavement,

      or on the counter,

      or in the dust,

of wounds apparent or invisible
of the inheritance one receives

      and numbly bequeaths in kind,

of the ancient inclination to turn away,
one supposes sin is innocent.

(1990)

IN DEFENSE OF DIRE ACTION

King Herod has his reasons, enjoys broad, general support
from the house, his counselors, who, after many sessions
of solemn debate, have come to agree, albeit without
pleasure, that this undertaking, if dire, is good governance,

that the very survival of order and of our trusted
modus operandi depends upon freeing the people
from this new challenge to global commerce and proper respect.
Granted, some will not agree, despite the call to put aside

petty differences, and to close ranks with those who must procure
with their swords our defense and stability. There are many who,
even now, give voice to treason at every opportunity
in both temple and marketplace, attempting

to subvert this just, protective action. Mark them. Their motives
are suspect, to say the least. Despite abundant evidence,
they refuse to see that one approaches, obscured by desert
wilderness, and makes his move against us. If allowed

to pursue ambition unchecked, he will one day surely turn
against our custom, against our rightful king, bring down
this nation, which, chosen of Providence, flourishes now, as a grip
of bright petals among thorns, as a gathering of lights.

Though he hide behind a sea of innocents, we must have him.

(1990)

AN END TO WINTER

In the interest of what desired return
do we lift the gauze of late winter dawn

from the stark field, lift our eyes to the one
blank disk rising above the ridge, upon

this ice-combusted field, as if to burn
away the drape of death held before the sun?

To what end shall we invest the field
when the great debris of past yields

lie sunken, collapsed beneath a hard
and unrelenting weather? Better, perhaps,

to focus somewhat less on likely outcome.
Better, perhaps, to rise and set to work.

(1990)

THE MARRIAGE BED
—for Marcia

Good to be so welcomed late in the day,
when so much of the day has been largely
unwelcoming, a little begrudging.

The children secure in their beds, the house
itself tucked in, the bed ample and warm,
good to let the day's resistances fall to the floor.

Good to find someone else willing that all
the lesser passions be replaced, or burned
away by more sacramental interest.

(1991)

SPEAKING OF DREAMS

A bad idea, generally, to discuss
one's dreams, laden as they are with revelation
which even one's dullest acquaintances surely
recognize long before the dreamer does. Still,
I did have one—a dream—one in which I died,
and violently. Well, *two* dreams, both violent.

In the first, I was driving through St. Louis,
following my brother who lived there at the time.
He was in his Ford, I in my green Volkswagen.
We waited for a light to change, and while we waited
I chanced to look off to my left, to where the Mobil
filling station lay still, as in a dream. I saw

the man with the gun taking money from the drawer
inside the luminous office. I saw him shoot
the boy whose dark, greased hands reached out. I saw him fall
clear out of being human—he was a bag of leaves then, the kind
you fill full as you can then put out for sanitation crews.
Well, this one wasn't tied right, and when it tipped it poured

a wash of leaves across the floor. And then the gunman
looked up at me. He must have known what I had seen.
He raised his gun as I glanced one more time ahead.
The light turned green. I waved my brother on. I heard
the window roar against my ear, and noticed,
as I died, how the change seemed oddly promising.

Unlikely as that one looks from here, the second dream
appears more troubling still, downright apocalyptic—
just the worst kind of revelation, the kind
that may let you imagine you've got this dreamer
pegged as one of those whose Christianity needs
a host of burning sinners in a burning lake

in order to find acceptable pleasure in paradise.
Well, wrong. It wasn't anything like that. Not at all.
I cleared the ridge-top just in time to meet the flash,
a brilliance racing from the east, and, here again,
I felt myself lean forward as if willing, even
that the blazing irresistible would soon arrive.

(1995)

MEDIOCRITY

No doubt, our making
      the most of meager
circumstance can pass
      for something very
like a virtue, like
      deep humility
and yes, beyond doubt
      our eager applause
despite the muddled
      school performance is
evidence of broad
      good will. Still, one might

wince at how often

        each feels thus obliged

to honor the thin

        custom of so much

being made of so

        very little, no?

(1996)

ALL SAINTS COMMUNION

Having accepted from the one palsied priest the cool,

the lucent wafer, having dipped it duly in the cup,

I pressed that sweet enormity fast against my tongue,

where on its sudden dissolution, I received a taste

of whose I was. I rose again and found my place.

As I knelt and tried to pray, I heard a little differently

the words the priest intoned as he continued offering

wheat passed for bread among high Protestants. His words:

The body of Christ, repeated as he set that emblem

in each cupped pair of outstretched hands. My eyes were shut,

so each communicant returning down the aisle became

something of a shadow illustration of the words. In that

fraught moment, they became as well absorbed into the vast

array of witnesses, whose cloud invisibly attended

our sacramental blurring of the edge that keeps us separate.

(1996)

ANAPHORA FOR ELLÁDA

—χωρίς συμπέρασμα

As my heart has fed since youth
      upon her pagan and her Christian myths

As I receive from her
      both my Hades and my Paradise

As my own dim regions and my light
      are drawn by her appearances

As of late the salt of the Aegean
      is what I savor most upon my lips

As her murmur is the sound
      that draws me in my dreams

As her thyme and grape and goat path
      cense my evening saunter

As her sainted earth is where I one day
      will lie down

(2004)

ORVIETO: DUOMO SWALLOWS

Of course they cannot mean to be
so beautiful. They mean only
to be fed, and so they fly,

earnestly engage their giddy
aerobatics overhead
with little thought, presumably,

---

to the wrought enormity

that works its Gothic ornament

well into their sheer domain,

with even less concern for how

they seem to us, thus entertained

by their evening spectacle,

their patent skill, and apt display

of how an honest hunger might

result in pure pursuit. I hope one day

to be just so inclined, to move

as quickly to what quickens me—

with so little thought, beautifully.

—for John Skillen

(2006)

POSTCARD FROM WALLACE STEVENS IN HEAVEN

I am very pleased—exceedingly, and even now—to find
my final days' conversion remains *allegéd* merely.

My favorite phrase: "alleged deathbed conversion."

If anything, it is the death itself that is alleged, and unconvincing.

(2006)

EPITHALAMION

—for Elizabeth and Steven

The children have been cornered and well scrubbed.
The elders have arisen from their naps.
The scattered clans and our most likely friends
have all arrived exhibiting a calm
and—let's face it—a rare sobriety.

For her—beloved of my very soul—
whose face since infancy has sometimes torn
my heart with worry, only to repair
that wound with deep, expanding gratitude,
I pray that she and her good Steven find

in one another, in the crucible
of human love, some fixed sign, manifest,
that witnesses to each an evening balm
to mend our troubled human circumstance,
a calm to still the tumult of the day.

In our keen eagerness that all goes well,
we've turned uniquely earnest as we pray
that these two young belovéds share a most
blessed journey, now and ever, and that we
may all remain complicit in their joy.

(2009)

EVENING INTERROGATIONS

—μετά την Ανάσταση του Χριστού

Why despite the God's famous and appalling
intercession does the earth still fail
to recover? Why do all its creatures look
to rush unchanged and, for all appearances,
eagerly into heedless bleak demise?

And as for you? Why, O beloved mediocrity,
do you continue—near as I can figure—to avert
your eyes from the troubled road ahead though surely
that road has become no less perilous of late?

You plod right steadily down a lane whose nature
you won't so much as entertain. And I? Well,
I have taken to sitting whenever possible
by the sea, where its salt breeze and fine salt spray
have occasion, very nearly, to awaken me.

Evenings—I should say—are best for this, given
how so much of the day has come to resemble,
albeit subtly, late evening, as all I see tilts
tipping into gathering dusk. This dimming, then,
this *evening*, will serve as likely microcosm
of our moment, which moment mingles all that has
preceded us into one neat grip let go.

But I was saying—I was *asking* why so great
an agency as *Life* so grandly introduced
into our matter has yet to manifest
anything like uniform reprieve from death.

I'm still asking. What, one has to wonder, remains
yet lacking in the sufferings of Christ? And what
is to be done? While I'm certain that the sea
is saying something—so to speak—I never quite
approximate its terms mid these dim shallows of
my seat among the ferns. Meantime, I must confess,
for all their nagging reticence and roiling mess,
these many provocations please exceedingly.

(2010)

FURTHER POSSIBLE ANSWERS
TO PRAYER

And as for hell, hell is deep chagrin, still
a deeply wrenching circumstance, if one
in which the soul no longer manages
to skirt what's what. The fire? Well, belovéd,
that rich searing is my tenderness, just
as felt by all who have for so long worked
to mute my tenderness, render it moot.
The only demons then in play will be
those you've carried with you, what cohort you
have wed, and fed, whose offspring you have borne.
Acute chagrin, then, which the soul, so long
as she is willing—so long as she does
not refuse—may one day simply shed.

(2010)

THIS THE MORNING

This is the Month, and this the happy morn
Wherein the Son of Heav'ns eternal King,
Of wedded Maid, and Virgin Mother born,
Our great redemption from above did bring . . .

—*"On the Morning of Christ's Nativity" by John Milton*

The issue is, of course, to apprehend

how time's allegéd passing fails to hold

sufficient grip on what does not depend

upon our *moment*. The timeless will not fold

quite so neatly into *now* and *then*,

but spans a space, vertiginous, and we

may of an instant become likewise drawn

into a mode of being where we see.

Which is to say, His coming *now*, this day

is likely to be figured best as prime

occasion to observe the truth that we

dwell likewise in a realm outside of time.

As we lean into prayer this year, let's say

as one: *Come Christ God, come this very day*.

(2011)

INDEX OF TITLES

ABOUT PARACLETE PRESS

Who We Are

Paraclete Press is a publisher of books, recordings, and DVDs on Christian spirituality. Our publishing represents a full expression of Christian belief and practice—from Catholic to Evangelical, from Protestant to Orthodox.

We are the publishing arm of the Community of Jesus, an ecumenical monastic community in the Benedictine tradition. As such, we are uniquely positioned in the marketplace without connection to a large corporation and with informal relationships to many branches and denominations of faith.

What We Are Doing

Paraclete Press Books

Paraclete publishes books that show the richness and depth of what it means to be Christian. Although Benedictine spirituality is at the heart of all that we do, we publish books that reflect the Christian experience across many cultures, time periods, and houses of worship. We publish books that nourish the vibrant life of the church and its people.

We have several different series, including the best-selling Paraclete Essentials and Paraclete Giants series of classic texts in contemporary English; Voices from the Monastery—men and women monastics writing about living a spiritual life today; award-winning poetry; best-selling gift books for children on the occasions of baptism and first communion; and the Active Prayer Series that brings creativity and liveliness to any life of prayer.

Mount Tabor Books

Paraclete's newest series, Mount Tabor Books, focuses on liturgical worship, art and art history, ecumenism, and the first millennium church, and was created in conjunction with the Mount Tabor Ecumenical Centre for Art and Spirituality in Barga, Italy.

Paraclete Recordings

From Gregorian chant to contemporary American choral works, our recordings celebrate the best of sacred choral music composed through the centuries that create a space for heaven and earth to intersect. Paraclete Recordings is the record label representing the internationally acclaimed choir Gloriæ Dei Cantores, praised for their "rapt and fathomless spiritual intensity" by *American Record Guide*; the Gloriæ Dei Cantores Schola, specializing in the study and performance of Gregorian chant; and the other instrumental artists of the Gloriæ Dei Artes Foundation.

Paraclete Press is also privileged to be the exclusive North American distributor of the recordings of the Monastic Choir of St. Peter's Abbey in Solesmes, France, long considered to be a leading authority on Gregorian chant.

Paraclete Video

Our DVDs offer spiritual help, healing, and biblical guidance for a broad range of life issues including grief and loss, marriage, forgiveness, facing death, bullying, addictions, Alzheimer's, and spiritual formation.

Learn more about us at our website:
www.paracletepress.com or phone us toll-free at 1.800.451.5006

SCAN
TO
READ
MORE

MORE PARACLETE POETRY

Prayers of a Young Poet
Rainer Maria Rilke
Translated by Mark S. Burrows
ISBN: 978-1-61261-076-4, $23.99, Hardcover

This volume marks the first translation of these prayer-poems into English. Rilke wrote them originally in 1899 upon returning to Germany from his first trip to Russia. There, he found himself entranced by Orthodox churches and monasteries, and above all by the icons that seemed to him like flames glowing in dark spaces. He intended these poems as icons of sorts, gestures that could illumine a way for seekers in the darkness.

Practicing Silence: New and Selected Verses
Bonnie Thurston
ISBN: 978-1-61261-561-5, $19.99, Paperback

"The old desert monks insisted that staying in one's cell would teach you everything. Bonnie Thurston shares, in finely crafted language, what she has learned in these deeply contemplative poems welling up from her own solitude. It is sheer grace to receive the fruit of her own spiritual journey."
—Lawrence S. Cunningham, The University of Notre Dame

Eyes Have I That See
John Julian
ISBN: 978-1-61261-640-7, $18.00, Paperback

From rough folk-verse to high-flown poesy, from a nine-line rhyme to a six-hundred-line epic, both the style and genre of the poetry in this volume cover a broad range of poetic possibility. This is the first volume of John Julian's poetry ever published, revealing an important new American poetic voice.

Available from most booksellers or through Paraclete Press:
www.paracletepress.com | 1-800-451-5006
Try your local bookstore first.